An Introduction to Classroom Observation

'A deeply insightful book, a great education and an intrepid defender of teachers and their professional expertise and dignity. Ted Wragg speaks with clarity, showing how difficult ideas and perspectives can be put across in ordinary language which all can understand. If you are puzzled about rating scales, static sampling, interaction analysis, triangulation, phenomenology or ethnomethodology, then you would do well to start here.'

Professor Richard Pring, University of Oxford, **UK**

How does classroom observation support your professional development? How can you observe as effectively as possible?

Highly regarded as one of the most widely used and authoritative texts on this topic, *An Introduction to Classroom Observation* is an essential text for anyone serious about becoming a good teacher or researcher in education.

Now part of the *Routledge Education Classic Edition Series*, E.C. Wragg's straightforward guide includes a combination of case studies, photographs and illustrations to show how various people study lessons for different purposes and in different contexts. It outlines a range of approaches in clear language and gives examples of successful methods that have been employed by teachers, student teachers, researchers and pupils.

With a new preface from Professor Richard Pring, the classic edition of this indispensable text is for a new generation of education professionals looking to become effective observers in the classroom.

E.C. Wragg was Professor of Education at the University of Exeter, UK. He was one of the finest international experts on research into teaching and learning, and always wrote with the teacher in mind. A regular columnist in the *Times Educational Supplement* and the *Guardian*, he was in demand for radio and TV education features. The Ted Wragg Teaching Award for Lifetime Achievement honours his memory, and is given annually to educators who are considered to have shown excellent devotion to teaching throughout their careers.

Routledge Education Classic Edition Series

The Routledge Education Classic Edition Series celebrates Routledge's commitment to excellence in scholarship, teaching, and learning within the field of education. Written by experts, these books are recognised as timeless classics covering a range of important issues, and continue to be recommended as key reading for education students and professionals in the area. With a new introduction that explores what has changed since the books were first published, where the field might go from here, and why these books are as relevant now as ever, the series presents key ideas to a new generation of educationalists.

Also available:

Apple, *Education and Power* (1982, second edition published 1995)

Drummond, *Assessing Children's Learning* (1993, second edition published 2007)

Gipps, *Beyond Testing* (1994)

Kincheloe, *Teachers as Researchers* (1991, second edition published 2002)

Powell and Jordan, *Autism and Learning* (1997)

Smith, *Understanding Reading* (1971, 1978, 1982, 1989, 1994, sixth edition published 2004)

Swanwick, *Teaching Music Musically* (1999)

Tripp, *Critical Incidents in Teaching* (1993)

Wragg, *An Introduction to Classroom Observation* (1993, second edition published 1999).

An Introduction to
Classroom Observation

Classic Edition

E. C. Wragg

Routledge
Taylor & Francis Group

LONDON AND NEW YORK

First published 1994
by Routledge

Second edition published 1999

This classic edition published 2012
by Routledge
2 Park Square, Milton Park, Abingdon, Oxon OX14 4RN

Simultaneously published in the USA and Canada
by Routledge
711 Third Avenue, New York, NY 10017

Routledge is an imprint of the Taylor & Francis Group, an informa business

© 1994, 1999 E. C. Wragg
© 2012 Preface, Richard Pring

British Library Cataloguing in Publication Data
A catalogue record for this book is available from the British Library

Library of Congress Cataloging in Publication Data
Wragg, E.C. (Edward Conrad)
An introduction to classroom observation/Ted Wragg. —Classic ed.
    p. cm.
Includes bibliographical references and index.
1. Observation (Educational method) 2. Teachers—Training of. I. Title.
LB1731.6.W73 2012
370.71'1—dc23
2011035945

ISBN: 978-0-415-68849-9 (hbk)
ISBN: 978-0-415-68850-5 (pbk)
ISBN: 978-0-203-35727-9 (ebk)

Typeset in Times New Roman
by RefineCatch Limited, Bungay, Suffolk

MIX
Paper from
responsible sources
FSC
www.fsc.org   FSC® C004839

Printed and bound in Great Britain by
TJ International Ltd, Padstow, Cornwall

Contents

Figures

Preface

I once observed a French lesson, part of which was taught entirely in French, with plenty of rapid-fire interaction between teacher and pupils. I was studying individual pupils in the class, so I kept note of who answered the teacher's questions. After the lesson I asked the teacher to say roughly how many pupils had given an oral answer to her questions. 'Oh, I don't know, there were lots of hands in the air,' she replied, 'I think most of them did. About twenty to twenty-five, was it?' The answer was eight. Perhaps it seemed like a lot more, but eight pupils, mainly sitting in the centre of the classroom, had actually responded. Careful classroom observation can help illuminate even the most familiar of events.

Observing the behaviour of our fellow humans is something we all start in babyhood and never finish until they finally screw the lid down on us. It is one of those taken-for-granted activities that occurs every day of our lives, in work, in the family, and in social situations. Much of what we see is repeated versions, with variations, of what we have observed many times before. It is because we have crossed the road thousands of times that we know what to look for, though the context will be different on each new occasion. We have the means of recognising what is familiar and what is novel, and this puts us in a position to make decisions rapidly about the speed of vehicles, their distance away, likely position in a few seconds, our own capability of walking or running at a certain pace and in a particular direction. Without the powers of observation and deduction most of us would have been dead years ago.

So if we already know all about our daily lives, why should we bother to hone the skills of observation? There are many reasons. First of all we may delude ourselves about what is happening. We often 'observe' what we want to see: harmonious relationships, effective practice, rules that are consistently followed. We may ignore or overlook what we don't wish to see: disjunction, ineffectiveness, unruliness. I have seen thousands of lessons and read accounts of many more, yet often when I go into this familiar school environment, alongside all the events that appear to resemble countless other similar happenings, I still, from time to time, notice something different. Classrooms are places that are capable of unfolding both familiarity and novelty. Even watching a tedious lesson is a challenge.

In fact, I sometimes find I am more busy in a boring lesson than an exciting one, because there are so many possibilities to explore.

Day after day millions of children and their teachers rehearse well known rituals, each with minor unique variations. Teaching strategies can be varied and adapted, yet some teachers make few changes to their established routines, and others keep the excitement of discovering new ways to help children learn throughout their career. This book is written in an attempt to make the business of classroom observation important, for trainee teachers, seasoned practitioners, for those responsible for training or supporting teachers or running schools, or for anyone who may want to look at what happens in a classroom with a more practised eye. Skilfully done, classroom observation can be a valuable tool for improving the quality of teaching; badly handled, it can be a menace. The first edition of *An Introduction to Classroom Observation* became a widely used book and I hope that this revised second edition will also help both beginners and experienced professionals explore more skilfully some of the infinite and subtle variations in classroom interaction and behaviour.

Acknowledgements

I have worked in the field of classroom observation since the mid-1960s, and trying to thank all the people from whom I have learned would take a lot of space. I would, however, like to express my gratitude to Ned Flanders, who helped me a great deal when I first started doing research in classrooms; to Sara Delamont, David Hamilton, George Brown, Ed Stones and many others who were stimulating company at seminars when all of us felt that we were working in the dark; to my colleagues at the Universities of Nottingham and Exeter, too numerous to mention; to the Leverhulme Trust in particular, and other funding bodies, for grants to study primary teaching, teacher appraisal, the improvement of literacy, classroom competence and other topics on teaching and learning; to the members of my research team, Gill Haynes, Caroline Wragg, Rosemary Chamberlin and Felicity Wikeley, skilful observers of thousands of lessons.

Preface to the classic edition

> Observing the behaviour of our fellow human beings is something we all start in babyhood and never finish until they finally screw the lid down on us.

In this opening sentence of the second paragraph of this excellent introduction to classroom observation, Ted Wragg could have been talking about himself, for he was 'the great observer'. Despite the demanding task of directing the largest university department of education in Britain apart from the London Institute of Education, there was hardly a week when he was not in a school, teaching the children, working with the teachers and, above all, observing with his unique insight what was going on.

This book, therefore, is much more than the theoretical reflections on research methods by an academic. There are many of those for sale. Rather is it a deeply insightful account of a great educator and an intrepid defender of teachers and their professional expertise and dignity. To fully understand this book, the reader needs to realise that it is driven by a passion for teaching and for enabling teachers to improve their teaching by becoming themselves the researchers. Academics have a part to play but, in Ted Wragg's view, a part which is subordinate to the real *dramatis personae*, the teachers in the classroom.

In arguing that, Ted Wragg was a powerful voice in a growing tradition of teachers as researchers, persuasively articulated by Lawrence Stenhouse in his 1975 *Introduction to Curriculum Research and Development*. There is no curriculum development without teacher development. It is important to be reminded of this at a time when the professional expertise and role of the teacher are continually being undermined, not simply by the interventions of Government and its agencies, but particularly by the Orwellian 'newspeak' of performance management, in which teachers have come to be seen as 'deliverers of the curriculum' – a curriculum created and packaged outside the classroom. Ted Wragg would have none of that. Teachers are the curriculum thinkers, not the 'deliverers'.

However, that thinking requires close observation of the pupils, their behaviour, their interactions, their relationships. And observation, to be free as possible from bias and to provide reliable evidence, requires skill as well as wisdom. This book therefore, when first published in 1994, aimed to do precisely that. It grew out of his own well illustrated work which he conducted over many years, together with an extensive reading of the literature on research methods. This literature often clouds rather than illuminates the practice about which it is written. But here Ted Wragg, 'the great communicator', speaks with clarity, showing how difficult ideas and perspectives can be put across in ordinary language which all can understand. If you are puzzled about rating scales, static sampling, interaction analysis, triangulation, phenomenology or ethnomethodology, then you would do well to start here. The ample illustrations show clearly the relevance to good observation as well as how that might take place within the classroom.

However, for Ted Wragg the whole world was but a classroom – adult learners as well as children – and the object of his shrewd observation. And these observations were weekly set out in his column for *The Times Educational Supplement*. Those observations had Ministers and Secretaries of State on edge as they revealed both to themselves and to teachers the reality of the political world and its impact upon schools and their classrooms. The classrooms observed could not be fully understood outside the ideological framework of our political masters. Once when the Secretary of State, Sir Keith Joseph, addressed the local Conservative Party, which had hired the lecture hall at the Exeter University School of Education (the former St Lukes College), Ted asked me to accompany him to the projection room overlooking the rostrum. There we could secretly observe Sir Keith defend, against the vociferous opposition of the local party, the professional right of teachers to have Campaign for Nuclear Disarmament stickers on their cars. It was a masterful defence by a passionate believer in freedom of opinion and expression, even when the opinions expressed were contrary to his beliefs. The episode, carefully observed, emerged in the warm 'obituary' given of Sir Keith's stewardship upon the latter's retirement. But the dangers of secret observation did not emerge until several years later. Having addressed a conference at Wolfson College Oxford along with Keith Joseph, I was seated next to him at dinner. After the soup, he turned to me and demanded sternly if my name was Pring. Feeling obliged to admit to this fact, he then admonished me for spying on him with Ted Wragg from a cubby hole in the lecture hall. I was able to deny this accusation because the projection room was no cubby hole. But such casuistry failed to deceive, though he remained pleased with the outcome of the observation as that had been reported by Ted Wragg. None the less, this third edition of *Classroom Observation* might well have had a brief addendum on the dangers and possible outcomes of 'secret observations'.

Professor Richard Pring, University of Oxford, UK
June 2011

Chapter 1

An introduction to classroom observation

'What sort of classroom observation shall we do?' This question is increasingly asked, when research into teaching and learning is undertaken, but it is also an issue discussed before the appraisal of experienced teachers, the training of novices or the inspection of schools. Nor is it only an issue for professional people. Parents, for example, may be invited into schools to see some teaching, as many schools have open days when visitors can watch what is happening in lessons. Classrooms are still relatively private places, but they are more open to scrutiny than they used to be. A great deal of money is spent on educating the next generation of citizens, consequently many people have a right to know what is going on in classrooms, where so much important teaching and learning takes place, even though children may learn from a variety of other sources.

Classrooms are exceptionally busy places, so observers need to be on their toes. Every day in classrooms around the world billions of events take place: teachers ask children questions, new concepts are explained, pupils talk to each other, some of those who misbehave are reprimanded, others are ignored. Jackson (1968) reported a study in which it was found that primary teachers engaged in as many as 1,000 such interpersonal exchanges in a single day. This means, if the pattern is repeated, 5,000 in a week, 200,000 in a year, millions in a professional career. In another study of videotapes by Adams and Biddle (1970), there was a change in 'activity' every 5–18 seconds and there was an average in each lesson of 174 changes in who talked and who listened. The job of teaching can be as busy as that of a telephonist or a sales assistant during peak shopping hours.

Yet despite greater openness to scrutiny, in many classrooms the craft of teaching is still largely a private affair. Some teachers spend 40 years in the classroom, teaching maybe 50,000 lessons or more, of which only a tiny number are witnessed by other adults. It is often difficult to obtain detailed accounts of lessons, because teachers are so busy with the running of the lesson there is little time for them to make notes or photographic records. I once went to a rural primary school and observed some of the most exciting science work I have ever seen. When I urged the teacher to write up what he was doing so that others could read about it, he declined, saying that his colleagues might think he was boasting. By contrast practice in surgery is a much more open matter. The developers of transplant and bypass surgery took it for granted that successful new techniques must be witnessed by and disseminated to others, through their actual presence at operations, or by means of videotapes and the written and spoken word.

Classroom observation is now becoming far more common than it once was. The advent of systematic teacher appraisal and lesson evaluation, the greater emphasis on developing the professional skills of initial trainees, or honing those of experienced practitioners, the increased interest in classroom processes by curriculum developers, all of these have led to more scrutiny of what actually goes on during teaching and learning. It is much more likely now, compared to the mid-1970s or even the mid-1980s, that one person will sit in and observe the lessons of another as part of a teacher appraisal exercise, or that a teacher supervising a student will be expected to make a more detailed analysis of lessons observed than might once have been the case.

If lessons are worth observing then they are also worth analysing properly, for little purpose is served if, after a lesson, observers simply exude goodwill, mumble vaguely or appear to be uncertain why they are there, or what they should talk about. The purpose of this book, therefore, is to describe the many contexts in which lessons are observed, discuss the purposes and outcomes of observation, the different approaches to lesson analysis, and the uses that can be made of the careful scrutiny of classroom events. There is now a huge constituency of people who need to be aware of what is involved in lesson observation or how it might be conducted. These include teachers, heads, student teachers, inspectors, appraisers, researchers, curriculum developers and anyone else who ever sits in on a lesson with a serious purpose. Skilfully handled classroom observation can benefit both the observer and the person observed, serving to inform and enhance the professional skill of both people. Badly handled, however, it becomes counter-productive, at its worst arousing hostility, resistance and suspicion.

Purposes and uses of observation

Consider just a few of the many uses of classroom observation: a primary teacher is being observed by the school's language co-ordinator, who comes for the morning to look at what can be done in response to concern about the relatively low literacy levels of certain boys in the school; a secondary science teacher is watched by the head of department during a one and a half hour laboratory session as part of the science department's self-appraisal exercise; a student on teaching practice is seen by a supervising teacher or tutor; a maths lesson is scrutinised by an inspector during a formal inspection of the school; a class of 7 year olds is observed by a teacher who is also a textbook writer preparing a series of mathematics activities for young children; a researcher studying teachers' questioning techniques watches a secondary geography class, noting down the various questions asked by the teacher and the responses obtained.

All of these are watching lessons, yet their purposes and approaches are very diverse. The mathematics textbook writer might focus specifically on individual pupils to see how effectively they coped with different kinds of activities, whereas the appraisers might give much of their time to the teacher's questioning, explaining, class management, the nature of the tasks set, and pupils' learning. One might make detailed notes, take photographs and record the whole process on video. Another might write little down, but rather reflect on what could be discussed with the teacher later.

What is important in all these cases is that the methods of classroom observation should suit its purposes. There is little point, when observing a student teacher, for example, in employing all the paraphernalia of a detailed research project if a different structure would make more sense. The research project might be using extensive systematic observation of pupils' movements, whereas the student might be having class management problems, so the principal focus might be on why children appear to be misbehaving, what they actually do, how the teacher responds, and what might be altered in future to avoid disruptive behaviour. The observer might, therefore, concentrate on the tasks the children have been set or devised for themselves, incidents that reveal the relationships between teacher and pupils and among the pupils themselves, the nature of classroom rules, or the lack of them. The purpose, timing and context of an observation should largely determine its methods, and this book describes how a range of approaches can be employed to meet a variety of needs.

ACTIVITY 1

Look at the photograph (Figure 1.1). Imagine that the teacher is concerned that she always seems to be trapped at her desk, with about a third of the class, sometimes as many as a half, waiting in line to see her. Consider how you might analyse what is happening, what would be the focus of your observations, the nature of the written record you might keep of events and what you might discuss afterwards.

There are many points on which to focus in such circumstances. Sometimes the teacher has made the pupils too dependent on her, and they may simply want to know how to spell words, when they might easily use a dictionary. The observer might look for examples of dependency so that these could be discussed later.

Focus of observation	Written record needed	Discussion points

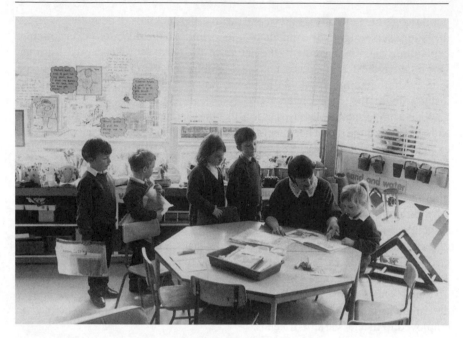

Figure 1.1 Children queuing at teacher's desk

The elements of the classroom

One of the problems faced by both experienced and inexperienced classroom observers is the matter of deciding what should be the focus of attention. So much happens in classrooms that any task or event, even apparently simple ones, could be the subject of pages of notes and hours of discussion. The ecology of many classrooms can be extremely rich and full. The main constituents of them are teachers, pupils, buildings and materials.

Teachers are the paid professionals, expected in law to act as a thoughtful parent might, to be *in loco parentis*. In order to fulfil what the law calls the 'duty of care', therefore, teachers are given certain powers as well as responsibilities. They may from time to time, for example, give punishments to children who do not behave properly, or take action to prevent injury to a pupil. Teachers' own background, personality, interests, knowledge, intentions and preferences will influence much of what occurs, such as the strategies they employ in different situations, the timing and nature of their questions and explanations, their responses to misbehaviour, indeed what they perceive to be deviant behaviour.

During any one day teachers may fill a variety of roles in carrying out their duties. These can include not only the traditional one of *transmitter of knowledge*, but also others such as *counsellor* (advising pupils about careers, aspirations or problems), *social worker* (dealing with family issues), *assessor* (marking children's work, giving tests, writing reports), *manager* (looking after resources, organising groups, setting goals), even *jailer* (keeping in school reluctant attenders or checking up on possible truants). As classroom life can be busy and rapidly changing, some teachers may fulfil several of these roles within the same lesson.

Children may also play different roles during lessons, sometimes in accordance with what is expected and required by the teacher, on other occasions according to their own choice. They are expected to be *learners* of knowledge, skills, attitudes or behaviour. From time to time they may also be *deviants* (misbehaving, not doing what the teacher has asked), *jokers* (laughing, creating humour which may lighten or heighten tension), *collaborators* (working closely with others as members of a team or group), *investigators* (enquiring, problem solving, exploring, testing hypotheses) or even *servants* (moving furniture, carrying and setting up equipment). As was the case with teachers, their background, personality, interests, prior knowledge, intentions and preferences will influence much of what occurs. Furthermore they will often be conscious of other members of their peer group, especially in adolescence, and this too will sometimes form a powerful influence on what they do.

Teaching takes place in a huge variety of locations. In institutions like schools and colleges, there are usually box-shaped classrooms, with furniture arranged in rows or around tables. This may not be the case in subjects like physical education or dance, however, where learning may take place in an open space or outdoors. Nor is it necessarily the norm in adult education, which may be located in the factory, the retail shop or even in settings like clubs, hospitals and people's homes, where there may be considerable informality. Open plan areas in schools may be L-shaped, circular or constructed with some quite irregular arrangement of space. We may well, on relatively rare occasions, be able to sit down with architects when designing a new school and try to turn our aspirations into reality, but most teachers have been given little say over the classrooms in which they teach and may find the buildings influence the styles of teaching that are possible, rather than the other way round.

Even within the same building there may be different uses of the spaces available. Teacher A may have a room with desks laid out in rows, teacher B may prefer groups working around tables, and teacher C may do so much practical work and movement that neither of these arrangements is appropriate. One primary age child may spend each day as a member of a large group of eighty pupils of similar age in a three class open plan area, another may be in a small village school built in the nineteenth century with twenty pupils of different ages. All these ecological factors, some beyond the direct control of teacher or pupil, can affect the nature of classroom interaction.

When it comes to the materials which children and teachers use, the books and equipment, the same variety can be noted. Herbert (1967) spent two years studying a school which had been specially designed for team teaching; he found that the learning media being used included eleven forms of book and printed matter (e.g. textbooks, worksheets, periodicals), nine forms of reference book (dictionary,

Figure 1.2 Two contrasting classrooms

encyclopedia, atlas, almanac), five kinds of test (textbook test, teacher-made test, standardised test), nine sorts of contentless media (paper, paint, crayon, clay), eleven forms of flat graphics (charts, posters, diagrams, magnetic boards), nine types of three-dimensional media (globes, models, toys, mobiles) and thirteen kinds of visual or audio-visual equipment (overhead projector, slide viewer, television monitor, micro-projector). Nowadays he would have found even more additions, such as computers, word processors and interactive technology, like the CD-ROM, virtual reality, workstations where pupils search world-wide databases for information. Any of these learning media can be influential on teaching and learning styles, and some classroom studies focus exclusively on their use.

Different methods of observation

One result of the diversity of purposes, practices and locations is that several different styles of classroom observation have been developed over the years. Some are drawn from traditions which involve systematic measurement and careful control of the conditions under which observations take place. Others are based on the approaches developed by anthropologists studying tribal life. Some observers may be influenced by the context in which the lesson takes place and may concentrate on some specific aspect of the teaching of one particular subject, like science or English. This in turn may influence whether they adopt a quantitative approach, counting and recording individual events, or a qualitative style of observation, trying to look behind and beneath the mere frequencies. If a teacher felt that she was not involving enough pupils in oral work then the observer might keep a log showing each pupil who answered, whereas if she believed she should improve the way she explains to lower ability pupils, then focus might be on the transcript of an audio recording of actual moments when she explained something.

The origins of many of the common approaches to classroom observation lie in the earlier part of the twentieth century. Indeed, there were examples of systematic approaches even before this time, and some of the best known teachers in history wrote down analyses of their own teaching practices. In the fifth century DE Confucius stated in his *Analects*: 'I shall not teach until the pupils desire to know something, and I do not help unless the pupils really need my help. If out of the four corners of a subject I have dealt thoroughly with one corner and the pupils cannot then find out the other three for themselves, then I do not explain any more'. In Greece, in the second century DE, Dionysius of Thrace laid down the steps to be followed when teaching about a literary work. They included the need to explain figures of speech, historical references and the etymology of some of the words used, and to estimate the literary merit of the work they were reading. In Rome Cicero and Quintilian analysed teaching methodology in detail. Their prescriptions on delivering a lecture, or asking children to write sentences in the style of the writer being studied, were highly influential.

Quantitative methods

In the twentieth century educational research came strongly under the influence of the nineteenth-century French philosopher Auguste Comte, who argued that human thought proceeded through three stages: the theological, the metaphysical and finally the positive or 'scientific'. There was a strong belief that systematic observation and analysis could lead to social behaviour being predicted, as relationships between one event and another became clear. An example of subsequent systematic quantitative analysis is the study by Stevens (1912) of 100 random observations of lessons in which the focus was on the questions that teachers asked in a variety of subjects. It was found that teachers talked for about 64 per cent of the time and pupils for 36 per cent, and that two to four 'lower level' (i.e. largely requiring the recall of information) questions were asked each minute.

Much of the early quantitative work was done in the United States at a time when the 'recitation lesson', that is the formal presentation of information by the teacher standing at the front of the class, was standard. In the 1920s and 1930s there was a great deal of interest in 'attentiveness', and observers would sit at the front of the class scanning faces to see how many pupils were arguably paying attention to the teacher. This allowed profiles to be drawn up showing the high and low points of the lesson, which could be related to content matter, test scores or other measures to see when the teacher seemed to be most effective. These were crude studies, but they laid the foundation for later work.

It soon became apparent that talk was an important element of classroom life, and classroom observation switched strongly to focusing on what teachers and pupils said to each other. Early investigators concentrated on devising category systems to elicit what kind of talk the teacher engaged in; Withall (1949) drew up a seven category system consisting of three 'learner-centred' (reassuring, accepting, questioning) categories, three 'teacher-centred' (directing, reproving, justifying own actions) categories and one 'neutral' (repetition, administration) category. Already these category systems began to take on their own values, favouring certain acts by the teacher and deprecating others, and much of the work published was highly tendentious.

One very influential writer at this time was Robert Bales (1950), who actually conducted most of his own observations on small groups of adults. He devised a twelve category system which appealed to investigators studying classrooms, because it had such elements as 'agrees', 'gives opinion', 'asks for suggestion' and 'shows antagonism'. Each member of the group under observation was given a code number, the observers were trained until they reached a high level of agreement about which category they would assign to events, and what happened was noted down in sequence. All these became standard practice in later quantitative observation. His finding that ten to twenty different events might occur within a single minute of discussion influenced later work by writers such as Ned Flanders (1970). The ten category system devised by Flanders is described in Chapter 2, which deals more fully with quantitative methods, but one feature of it is that the observer records what is happening every three seconds.

Lying at the heart of the quantitative approach is a belief that the effectiveness of teachers can be improved if a body of knowledge is established which shows that they should do more of some things and less of others. Though this has an appeal, it has to be said that there are relatively few findings that can be said to be of wide general concern. There are some quantitative studies that are of general interest, such as the one by Jackson (1968) that teachers can engage in over 1,000 interpersonal transactions in a single day, by Brophy (1981) showing infrequent and haphazard use of praise, by Deutsch (1960) that some inner-city teachers in American schools spent up to 75 per cent of their day trying to keep order, by Rowe (1972) that teachers allowed on average one second between a pupil answer and their own statement, by Wragg (1993a) that 57 per cent of primary teachers' questions were related to class management, 35 per cent to information recall and only 8 per cent required a higher order of thinking.

However, Jackson (1962) summed up earlier work as 'so low in intellectual food value that it is almost embarrassing to discuss them'; even high quality recent work offers relatively little that is generalisable to all classrooms, though a great deal that is of interest to any individual curious to know whether what is reported elsewhere is also the case in his or her own teaching. The observation of individual teachers, therefore, can utilise some of the approaches of those who have devised good quantitative methods, albeit with caution, even if the eventual findings from them are not the same as those of the original investigator or category designer.

Qualitative methods

While the counting of events may offer some interesting insights, it falls far short of telling the whole story of classroom life. Consider the following statement: 'Andrew, haven't you started yet?' An analysis of the lesson that concentrated entirely on event counting might note that this was one of thirty-seven questions asked by the teacher during the lesson observed. In a category system it might be coded as 'managerial' or 'addressed to individual pupil'.

Yet suppose that the teacher was extremely exasperated with Andrew and that he uttered the words in a loud and rough voice, following it up with a punishment. This might provoke a reaction different from the one that would have followed a gentle chiding voice. Alternatively suppose that Andrew was a sensitive boy for whom one more reprimand was the final straw, as he felt the teacher always made him a target, but ignored other pupils' misbehaviour. Such context factors may override in importance the fact that the teacher's statement was the seventh of fifteen managerial questions.

The origins of some approaches to classroom observation that concentrate on the significance, meaning, impact, individual or collective interpretation of events, are rooted in a different tradition from that of the positivists described above. One strong influence is the work of cultural and social anthropologists; this style of observation is often given the generic label 'ethnographic'. It attempts to address the problem that most of us find with observing in a classroom, which is that it is such a familiar location. After all we have usually spent some 15,000 hours as pupils, many observers are themselves teachers, and it is easy to look straight through events that might hold significance, simply because we take them for granted, so we never really see them with a critical eye.

Anthropologists have to detach themselves from the familiar and, like intelligent Martians, probe behind the surface of what happens. If they arrive in some location where their assignment is to study the life in a particular tribe, they may initially understand little of what they see. However, by building up a picture of tribal life, noting down certain events, interviewing members to hear their explanations, matching one happening or explanation against others, they can soon establish a framework of understanding. A dance that appeared meaningless at first can be seen later as part of a series of rituals connected with fertility and growth, related to the planting of crops, the harvest, beliefs about the weather in general, or rainfall in particular.

Some of these approaches to the observation and understanding of human behaviour can be translated successfully into the study of classrooms. An observer might make notes about an event and then interview the participants afterwards, asking questions about who did what, and why. This then allows one to pool the perceptions of the people who witnessed what happened. Consider, for example, this exchange between a teacher and two 13 year old secondary pupils:

Teacher: What on earth do you think you're doing? (*in response to geometry instruments falling noisily on the floor*)
Lila: I was just borrowing Marion's ruler.
Teacher: Well why are you making such a fuss about it?
Marion: It fell on the floor.
Teacher: I didn't ask you. You can both stay in for half an hour at lunch time.

In interview afterwards the teacher said that he always took a firm line and would punish these two pupils if ever they misbehaved as an example to the rest, as they were, in his view, 'ringleaders' of a group of others. Lila and Marion, however, saw the same event differently. They would frequently wind the teacher up, they said in interview, even though they were a little apprehensive about what he might do. No one liked him, they explained, as he was too severe and was constantly carping about petty misbehaviour, so, by taking him on, they acquired heroic status in the eyes of others. Having to stay in occasionally at lunch time was a small price to pay. Further observations confirmed this pattern of abrasive interaction between the two friends and the teacher.

This is a good example of differing perceptions of the same events. Both the teacher and the pupils saw themselves as winning these regular confrontations: the teacher because he punished Lila and Marion for their misbehaviour, which usually meant it ceased or lessened for a while, the pupils because they defied his authority, which they regarded as enhancing their status in the eyes of their peers. Since both sides saw such exchanges as reflecting credit and success on their part, they were content for this pattern of interaction to continue. By observing the events and interviewing the participants the observer was able to fill out an interpretation of what was happening in the classroom that would not have been apparent from event counting alone. Chapter 3 describes such qualitative methods in more detail.

Other approaches

One interesting angle on classroom life comes from ethologists who have studied animal behaviour. This might seem a very appropriate or inappropriate perspective, depending on your view of children, but many colonies of creatures show interesting patterns of behaviour when younger and older members are together. Indeed, teaching and learning can often be witnessed, even though they may not take place in such formal institutions as schools. Certainly different kinds of social learning – knowing your place, respecting your elders, staying on your own territory and not straying on to that of others – take place regularly in animal communities.

Ethologists have often studied phenomena which can be witnessed in classrooms. The seminal book by Lorenz (1966) *On Aggression* is titled in the original German *Über das sogenannte Böse* (about the so-called 'evil'). It tries to look at the manifestations of aggression, like bared teeth or the bristling mane, and see how and why they occur. Pupils can sometimes be aggressive with each other,

Figure 1.3 Different interpretations of the same event – how do pupil and teacher see it?

pushing and shoving often taking place when children are jostling for facilities, perhaps trying to get to the computer or the science experiment first. This raises questions during classroom observation, like whether boys or girls as a group, or certain individual pupils, are more aggressive when it comes to securing equipment, materials or the teacher's attention, and how, if at all, the teacher responds.

Figure 1.4 Teaching and learning

The establishment and maintenance of dominance among animals has also been studied by ethologists, and this too has some relevance to classroom life, especially if one is studying class management. Infant teachers, who normally crouch alongside children when monitoring or discussing their work in order to minimise the height difference and reduce anxiety, may suddenly switch to maximising the difference in their height by towering over them if they are telling them off for misbehaviour.

The spoken word has often been a central focus during classroom observation, and it can be enhanced by variations in *voice*, when teachers use a loud or soft tone, emphasise certain words, or change from a high to a low pitch. However, although a great deal of attention has been given to what teachers and pupils say to each other in the classroom, there are important *non-verbal* aspects of classroom life that observers will often find of interest. Teachers often amplify an explanation with *gesture*, pointing a finger or spreading their arms, to make a point more clearly or emphatically. Another important element can be *movement*, when the teacher walks towards somebody or away from a group. *Body language* generally signals important messages, as when the teacher leans casually on the desk, or when a new teacher underlines his anxiety and uncertainty by holding his hands tightly under his armpits.

For observers wanting to conduct a detailed analysis of what is said in the classroom it is sometimes worth recording and transcribing a part of a lesson. Although a written transcript is time-consuming to compile and leaves out a great deal of what happened, especially the non-verbal aspects, it does allow much more detailed analysis of events than many other methods. Looking at the written record as soon after the event as possible allows teachers and observers to recall what happened in the lesson and discuss important aspects of classroom interaction.

ACTIVITY 2

Imagine you have just observed a lesson on the topic 'Insects'. Below is a transcript of the opening part of the lesson. Decide what you would want to discuss with the teacher.

Teacher: I'm going to give you the little word 'insect'. Immediately in your mind there's a picture of something, I expect. There is in mine. What sort of picture have you got Cassandra?

Pupil 1: A spider.

Teacher: OK, you think of a spider. You keep the spider there. Catherine, what about you?

Pupil 2: (*no response.*)

Teacher: When I say 'insect' what do you immediately think of – an insect?

Pupil 3: A ladybird.

Teacher: Yes, that's right.

Pupil 4:   A worm.

Teacher: Yes – anything else?

Pupil 3:   A snail.

Teacher: How do insects move around, Peter?

Pupil 2:   Legs.

Teacher: How many legs has an insect got?

Pupil 2:   Six.

Teacher: Yes, six, but do insects get around any other way?

Pupil 2:   Some insects fly.

Teacher: Yes, some insects use wings. Can you think of an insect that flies?

Pupil 2:   An eagle.

Teacher: An eagle? Is that an insect? No, it's a bird. A bird is definitely not an insect.

The outcome of this lesson was that most children were unclear what an insect actually was, as tests given to them afterwards revealed, and the teacher himself made a number of factual errors during the lesson. The availability of even a short piece of transcript means that the teacher and observer can focus on such matters as factual inaccuracies (a worm is not an insect), uncertainty (the teacher never indicates whether the answer 'snail' is correct or not) and the shape and structure of the explanation (the focus shifts from parts of the body to forms of locomotion for no apparent reason).

The observer

It has to be recognised that when someone new comes into a classroom to observe, then the very presence of an additional adult who is not normally present may itself influence what happens. It is not easy to say exactly how things might change, because this will depend on many factors, such as how common it is for visitors to arrive in the room, the status of the person concerned, even such matters as the age, dress and sex of the observer. The class of a student teacher might be unusually well behaved if the head teacher arrives to observe; a group of adolescent boys or girls in a single sex school might react differently depending on whether the observer is of the same sex as themselves; a class in an open plan school, well used to parent helpers, numerous unannounced visitors and the presence in the same area of more than one teacher, would be less likely to change its behaviour radically if an observer turned up one day, than a class in a school which rarely saw any strangers.

There have been studies of the effects of observers on classroom interaction. Samph (1976) planted microphones in classrooms and then sent observers either announced or unexpected some weeks later. He found that teachers made more use of questions, praise and were more likely to accept pupils' ideas when someone was present. Teachers and indeed pupils may attempt to provide what they think the visitor expects, and this will vary according to the impression or stereotype they form of the observer concerned. They may be irritated or excited by a visitor and behave differently from normal, hence the need for observers, where possible, to study a series of lessons rather than a single one.

Some observers are members of the school, often teachers in it. There are differences between what in the literature on classroom observation are called *participant* and *non-participant* observers. Insiders can sometimes find it difficult to detach themselves from their own prior knowledge, beliefs, commitments and prejudices about a place they know very well and have seen every day for years. On the other hand they often understand the significance of events that might elude strangers. Outsiders are sometimes able to be more emotionally detached about what they see, but may occasionally be bewildered by it, or even misinterpret events through their unfamiliarity.

It is important for non-participant observers to make sure they learn what they need to know by looking beneath the surface of what happens, and discuss their perceptions with others. It is equally valuable for participant observers to shed the worst of their pre-judgements, approach observation with an open mind and ask themselves what, if anything, might get in the way of their seeing things objectively. Even matters such as dress and positioning are worth thinking about. Most observers try to dress in a manner that will not draw attention to themselves and find some discreet position in a corner or at the back of a room, where their

'Remember to be discreet'

Figure 1.5 Classroom observation

presence will be less likely to affect events. Minimising the intrusion, not overplaying the 'status' card, making contact with the teacher beforehand, clarifying the purpose and likely outcome of the observation, all these are necessary if what is seen is to be as natural and unstaged as possible.

Recording the observation

Observers have some choices about what sort of record should be kept of a lesson, and some may choose to keep none at all. Most, however, will at least keep notes, but there are several other possibilities. Small compact video cameras and sound cassettes offer further options beyond written notes, though teachers and pupils who are not used to being video recorded may be inhibited. Each approach has advantages and disadvantages, and some of these are listed below:

Method	Advantages	Disadvantages
Written account	Immediate and fresh account available; economic use of time; account can be available for discussion immediately after lesson; full picture of events available to observer at time of observation.	Observer must make immediate decisions about what to record, so may be superficial or unreliable account; no chance of 'action replay'; some effects on class behaviour because of observer's presence
Video cassette	Good visual and sound record which can be replayed several times; no pressure to make instant decisions; focus can be on teacher only or on individual or group of pupils; lesson can be discussed with participants.	Loss of information such as room temperature, smells, events out of camera shot; effects on class of presence of camera; increase in time needed for analysis
Sound cassette	Good sound record can be replayed several times for discussion, analysis, or corroboration of written account; radio microphone can be used to obtain high quality record of what the teacher says; observer's comments can be recorded simultaneously on twin-track tape; allows lesson to be transcribed by audio typist.	Loss of important visual cues such as facial expressions, gesture, body language, movement; sound quality can be poor without radio microphone, especially if acoustics are poor; difficult to identify individual children who speak; analysis time substantially increased.
Transcript	Enables really detailed analysis at leisure; permits analysis by several people not necessarily in the same place, as text can be distributed easily; person being observed can work on specific aspects of language, such as choosing good examples of analogies, using an appropriate vocabulary	Loss of important visual and sound cues such as tone of voice, volume of noise, emphasis; high cost in time and money to have lessons transcribed (one lesson might fill twenty or thirty pages); difficulty of deciding what to focus on if numerous transcripts are collected.

Nonetheless, despite some of the difficulties of visiting classrooms and observing lessons, it is a worthwhile enterprise and one that should be undertaken in a thoughtful and professional manner. There is still a great deal to be learned by any teacher, novice or seasoned practitioner, or by any investigator. Good classroom observation can lie at the heart of both understanding professional practice and improving its quality.

In the remainder of this book I shall describe quantitative and qualitative approaches in Chapters 2 and 3 respectively; the use of classroom observation in specific contexts, such as teacher training, professional improvement and teacher appraisal, in Chapter 4; the place and use of observation in research and curriculum development in Chapter 5; and finally, in Chapter 6, I shall give additional examples of classroom observation in action.

Chapter 2

The use of quantitative methods

How long did the oral interaction part of the lesson last? How many pupils read to the teacher during the day? Did the girls or the boys in the class have more contacts with the teacher? How many questions asked by the teacher obtained a correct response, and which pupils gave correct and incorrect answers? There are many questions about quantities in classroom interaction, and consequently numerous ways of attempting to quantify what happens. Some observers use *rating scales*, others prefer some kind of *category system*. There are now thousands of published systems as well as unknown numbers of home-made approaches. Rather than gratefully seizing a category system or rating scale simply because it is available, it is better for observers to ask themselves *why* they might want to quantify something, as well as what might be the focus of their attention.

There are numerous instances when quantities can be informative, especially when these are related to intentions. If the teacher wants everyone to have a turn using a particular piece of equipment, like a computer, during a particular day, then it is useful to know whether all the class did in fact have an opportunity, or whether it was only a half or even a quarter of the pupils. It would also be valuable to know which pupils did and did not manage to obtain a turn, as well as more qualitative information, such as why some completed the assignment and others did not. Similarly, if a teacher believes that children should sometimes give longer answers, rather than short one-word replies, it is important to know how often this aspiration is fulfilled, and any explanation of the outcome. Quantitative and qualitative approaches need not be seen as polar opposites, as they can often complement each other.

Systematic analysis of lessons has often concentrated on a number of matters in the classroom. They include the following, some of which overlap with each other:

Personal traits   The traits of either the teacher or the pupils: for example, whether the teacher is warm or aloof, whether certain pupils appear to prefer collaboration or disruption.

Verbal interaction   What teachers and pupils say to each other, who does the talking and about what, question and answer, choice of vocabulary and language register.

Non-verbal	Movement, gesture, facial expression like smiles and frowns.
Activity	The nature of the pupils' tasks, what the teacher does.
Management	How the teacher manages pupil behaviour, the use of resources, the organisation of group or individual work.
Professional skills	Questioning, explaining, arousing interest and curiosity.
Teaching aids	The teacher's use of audio-visual aids, such as television, slides, tapes, or other materials and equipment, like the computer.
Affective	Teachers' and pupils' feelings and emotions, interpersonal relationships.
Cognitive	The nature and level of thinking in the classroom – for example, the level of reasoning necessary to answer a question, or the degree of understanding a pupil appears to have of a topic or concept.
Sociological	The roles people play, norms, codes, the effects of social background, status, power.

All of these aspects of classroom life can also be studied by qualitative methods, and indeed have been, especially such matters as relationships, emotional tone, the use or misuse of power, status. However, this chapter will concentrate on attempts to quantify what is witnessed, a matter which raises interesting philosophical and ideological issues. In order to determine and record how often or to what degree something happens, it is usually necessary to have decided in advance what is to be quantified. The main strength of this rational *a priori* view is that it allows the observer to concentrate on elements of classroom life according to procedures carefully worked out in advance. The weakness is that it is less easy to respond to the unexpected, or to retain the flexibility to follow one's judgement about what is important in the lesson in the light of actual events.

This philosophical dilemma is shown on the continuum below:

Preordained schedule ------------------------------------ *open-minded*

Compare two different classroom observers looking at the same issue, but from different standpoints.

Left on the continuum Let us suppose that teachers in a school are concerned about the amount of disruption from pupils who misbehave, so they want to see if they can reduce it. Observer A, operating towards the left-hand side of the continuum, might decide to watch classes of pupils counting up how many appear to be disruptive, noting who the disruptives are and what they do. It might be anticipated in advance that disruption often follows when children get out of their seat without permission and then distract others, so this could be one of the categories noted. The observation phase might then be followed by some kind of action programme during which teachers try to reinforce and recognise good behaviour whenever it occurs, or take out pupils who misbehave for special counselling. The observer might then go into the classroom after the programme using the same observation schedules as previously, to see if the incidence of misbehaviour had increased, decreased, or remained the same.

Right on the continuum   Observer B, operating towards the right-hand side of the continuum, by contrast, though clear about the focus on disruptive behaviour, would not determine explicit categories beforehand. It would be more likely that interviews would take place in advance of, or after observations, to determine what teachers and pupils regarded as disruptive and why. The observer might make extensive notes on incidents that occurred during lessons, and ask those concerned to explain how they saw these. The perceptions of different participants could then be brought together to find agreement or inconsistencies and some kind of action programme could be devised and evaluated in the light of how people interpreted events.

It would be easy to caricature the difference between the two approaches and claim that Observer A is rigorous and systematic, and Observer B slapdash and amateurish; or equally that Observer A is insensitive and mechanistic, whereas Observer B is thoughtful and profound. In reality the two are simply operating different strategies which they may or may not employ skilfully. It is a little like saying one wants a single 'true' account of someone's wedding. Does one choose a photograph, if so, which one? Would a video be better, or a first-hand account from someone present, or a list of factual information telling who got married to whom, where and when? Which single or multiple record suffices will depend on the circumstances and the wishes of the person seeking the account. It is perfectly possible to adopt a variety of approaches to classroom observation, as well as favour a single one.

Figure 2.1 Observing and interpreting disruptive behaviour

Rating scales

The use of rating scales in classroom observation was widespread a few years ago. Indeed, in many cases a list of ratings was the sole outcome. Typically pairs of bi-polar opposites, often based on assessment of the teacher's personality, were scored on a five, seven or even ten point scale. Some ratings focused more on manifest classroom traits, rather than individual personality features, and dimensions such as 'well prepared–badly prepared' were commonplace. Mostly the features of a rating schedule were based on commonsense assumptions, rather than the results of research, though Ryans (1960), in a substantial evaluation of teachers' characteristics, used traits that appeared to be related to 'success' in the classroom, like the ones below:

warm	1	2	3	4	5	6	7	aloof
stimulating	1	2	3	4	5	6	7	dull
businesslike	1	2	3	4	5	6	7	slipshod

This approach was criticised for a number of reasons, some self-evident, others more technical. The most frequent comment is that one rater's choice of scale point '4' may not mean the same as another rater's, though it is possible to train observers until they show quite high agreement with each other. Another set of criticisms applies to rating scales generally. The *halo effect* occurs when the rater is tempted to make a general judgement that the person concerned is a '2' or a '6' type person and award roughly the same grade on every scale. *Recency* is the tendency to be influenced by what has happened recently, giving the person a low rating on some trait such as 'businesslike' if something just happens to go wrong with the organisation of the lesson at the very moment when the observer is deciding the grade. *Central clustering* is often the result of uncertainty; it leads raters to score every event or person at points 3, 4 or 5 for fear of stepping out of line if they utilise the whole range.

Rating scales are often best employed by observers who will see many classrooms, as they are more likely to be able to build up experience at assigning the grades in different contexts, whereas those who see only one or two teachers may not be sure how to use a particular scale. Sometimes observers will use a measure of frequency, rather than intensity, and concentrate more on actual behaviour instead of personality. A typical scale might involve the rater in circling a number from 1 to 5 to indicate how often something seemed to happen in a lesson. The range might be 1 = never, or almost never, 2 = rarely, 3 = sometimes, 4 = often, and 5 = always, or almost always. The observer would then score items like the ones below using this scale.

Teacher praises correct answers	1	2	3	4	5
Teacher deals with misbehaviour	1	2	3	4	5
Pupils distract other children	1	2	3	4	5

In order to address questions about the subjectivity of rating scales, there is a development which attempts to relate categories to specific acts of behaviour. It is known as *Behaviourally Anchored Rating Scales (BARS)* and the numbers correspond to what teachers or pupils actually do on what is seen to be a rising scale of intensity or desirability. This approach is often preferred in the appraisal of employees in industry and commerce when the intention is to give feedback about performance which will steer people in a direction thought to lead to greater productivity or effectiveness. For example, on a ten point scale for sales managers, a low grade like 2 might have a cluster of items such as 'criticises sales assistants in front of customers' or 'acts unsympathetically when dealing with genuine complaints', whereas a high grade like 9 might include 'encourages commitment of sales staff by giving them responsibility' or 'arranges regular in-store training'.

An equivalent in the observation of teachers in classrooms is shown below. It might, in the case of a low grade on a dimension like 'pupil response', include 'children inattentive' or 'few responses to questions', whereas a high score would have items attached to it such as 'discussion of work often initiated by children themselves' or 'pupils appear disappointed when lesson ends'. The essential difference between this and the traditional rating scale is that the observer has plenty of clues about the criteria for each point on the scale, and it is not simply left to subjective judgement.

Behaviourally Anchored Rating Scale

Scale point   Typical behaviour

Scale point	Typical behaviour
1	Rare answers to questions; children inattentive; no real interest from class.
2	Only occasional answers; usually same three or four pupils; little interest.
3	About half the class appears to be engaged; several pupils answer teacher's questions; some pupils take the initiative and volunteer answers.
4	High degree of pupil interest and participation; many pupils take part, either in response to questions/commands or spontaneously.
5	Most or all pupils eager to join in; discussion of work often initiated by children themselves; pupils appear disappointed when lesson ends.

One of the major problems with rating scales is that they appear objective, but are in practice heavily laden with the values of those who conceived them. They can be misused, becoming a crude device for overriding teachers' individual professional judgement and making them strive to achieve the goals of their superiors, especially if the observation takes place in the context of assigning merit awards or carrying out appraisal.

An item like 'teacher sticks to lesson plan', for example, can be placed at the *hurrah!* or *boo!* end of a rating scale, depending on whether the deviser wants to encourage flexibility or rigidity. As an item, it is in itself neutral, for there can be occasions when teachers quite rightly keep close to their original intentions, and other times when to do so would be disastrous in the light of what actually happens in the lesson. It is often the context which determines the desirability or otherwise of a certain piece of behaviour. Rating scales, therefore, can be useful in classroom observation, but they arc best employed by experienced observers seeing numerous teachers, and they should never be used automatically, only when the context seems appropriate, and then with considerable caution.

Category systems

Rating schedules that require the observer to exercise considerable subjective judgement are often referred to as *high inference* measures. By contrast, *low inference* measures involve the observer much more in recording whether or not something took place. If someone wanted to see how healthy an environment a particular classroom offered, then a high inference approach would be to rate it on certain general features, such as 'cleanliness' or 'health-conscious behaviour'. A low inference approach, however, would concentrate on the occurrence of discrete pieces of behaviour thought to be associated with good or poor health, and could involve the observer noting down how often a pupil sneezed or coughed without using a handkerchief or covering his face, or whether children washed their hands after visiting the toilet.

ACTIVITY 3

Imagine you are going to study a teacher's class management with a view to compiling a record of how well children appear to *follow her classroom rules*, like 'raise your hands before answering a question' or 'don't leave your seat without permission'. Write down briefly the following:

1   How would you draw up and construct a high inference approach?
2   How would you draw up and construct a low inference approach?

In your response to Activity 3 you may well have devised a set of categories, in particular for your low inference approach. This is not always an easy matter, and there are a number of guidelines that are worth following. Take for example the question of pupils raising their hands to answer a question. It would be possible to use a category 'child raises hand' and then tick the name of any pupil who raises a hand when asking or responding to a question. This is a better approach than phrasing the category as a negative, like 'child fails to raise hand', as you would be recording a tick against most children's names every minute of the lesson, unless the context were specified. On the other hand a category such as 'pupil calls out without raising hand first' might be used to express something negative, because the first part is expressed in positive form 'pupil calls out . . .', so it would only involve recording those who did so, though this would not be a good category, as it combines two features, calling out and raising or failing to raise a hand first. A category description should, wherever possible, be unambiguous and easy to assign during what can be a busy observation period.

There are many common errors that are made when category systems are constructed, such as the following:

pupil happily reads book	(covers two types of category – 'action' and 'mood')
teacher shows interest	(too vague, target of interest not clear, better to qualify it)
pupil misbehaves and is told off	(two consecutive acts, should be coded separately)

In view of the difficulty of devising home-made categories, many observers prefer to use someone else's schedule. The classroom observation literature is now full of published category systems, some devised for research projects, others for teacher training or appraisal. However, even using a published system should involve a degree of reflection, rather than the uncritical application of an instrument constructed by someone with perhaps a quite different focus or purpose. Whether choosing a ready-made set of categories or devising one's own, there are several considerations which must be taken into account, such as the main purpose and focus, the sampling period, the nature of the record and the use to which the data will be put.

Specific focus

An observer watching a foreign language lesson in a secondary school might want to highlight quite different features from someone looking at a reception class in a primary school. The former might be concentrating on the oral parts of the lesson and so devise categories such as 'pupil answers teacher's question in the foreign language' or 'teacher gives command in the foreign language'. The latter might want to study social behaviour among children starting school, and so draw up headings like 'child snatches toy' or 'teacher praises good behaviour'.

One way of deciding the aspects of classroom interaction on which to focus is to undertake a pilot study of a few lessons in the field under observation and make notes, not only about events which catch the eye, but also about routine matters which can easily be taken for granted. Some classroom observers are influenced by a particular perspective or theoretical influence, so this will often partially determine the emphasis. Consider some of the following contexts and perspectives.

Science

If the observer wanted to see the extent to which the aims of a particular curriculum emphasising *investigation* were being fulfilled, then one matter of concern could be whether pupils did experiments, recorded their findings and discussed the

Figure 2.2 Science investigation lesson

outcome. Categories might include 'pupil makes hypothesis or speculates', 'teacher asks about findings' or 'pupil formulates scientific law or proposition'. The focus might be on what the pupils do, what the teacher does, or both. For example, there might be a category split into three options: 'Summary by teacher/ pupil(s)/both'.

Modern languages

Interest in the use of the foreign language in the classroom could produce a set of categories that were identical for the native and foreign language parts of the lesson, with a special code or suffix for the latter, for example:

4   Teacher asks question in English
4a Teacher asks question in the foreign language
6   Teacher gives command in English
6a Teacher gives command in the foreign language
8   Pupil answers in English
8a Pupil answers in the foreign language
9   Pupil asks question in English
9a Pupil asks question in the foreign language

Physical education

An observer might want to see how active different children are in physical education lessons. A log of individual children's activities could be constructed with categories such as 'runs slowly', 'runs quickly', 'jumps', 'uses piece of gymnastic apparatus (specify which)', 'plays ball'; this might then be related to other measures of activity, like the monitoring of heart rates during exercise. There will be further description of projects of this kind, linking different quantitative measures, in Chapters 4, 5 and 6.

Behaviour modification

Someone influenced by behaviourist learning theory (Skinner 1954) and wanting to apply it in the classroom would want to ensure that the principles were applied in a consistent manner. According to the tenets of behaviourism the teacher should ignore misbehaviour, on the grounds that this will lead to its extinction (an assumption by no means wholly agreed among practitioners) and reinforce 'good' behaviour, so that this will occur more frequently. Categories might include, therefore, 'teacher praises pupil' as well as different types or degrees of what is perceived to be misbehaviour, such as 'illicit talk', 'movement without permission' or 'physical aggression towards another pupil'.

This kind of programme is often controversial, and the use of category systems alone is usually insufficient to evaluate it properly. For example, it is easy to demonstrate whether the incidence of misbehaviour is reduced after an action programme, but figures about the degree of decline do not, by themselves, address questions of value, such as the effect of the programme on pupils and teacher. An action programme to reduce children fidgeting during lessons might well appear to 'work', in the sense that a count of instances of children being restless might show a decline by the end of the programme. However, if children shuffled in their seats because the lessons were tedious and did not arouse their interest, then valuable cues about boredom have simply been obliterated. Only symptoms, rather than causes, have been addressed, and the teacher may have been given a licence to bore. Nonetheless, if used intelligently, quantitative data can be an important part of an analysis.

Reading

A teacher might want to know how frequently she hears individual pupils read. An individual pupil log filled in by an observer, therefore, could offer categories such as 'teacher calls out pupil to hear reading' or 'pupil solicits teacher's attention to hear reading'. Another focus, however, might be on what the teacher does when the child makes a mistake when reading out loud. In this case the observer may have a category 'pupil makes error' (which in turn could be subdivided into types of error), followed by others like 'teacher ignores', 'teacher corrects', 'teacher asks child to try again' or 'teacher points to error without speaking'. This would allow the observer to build up profiles of miscues, showing how the teacher responds when children make different kinds of mistakes in their reading.

Creativity

Although some teachers or observers want to concentrate on a particular subject or type of classroom activity, others might wish to address a more overarching notion like 'creativity', or the extent to which children are able to use their imagination and ingenuity, irrespective of the subject being taught. In this case there could be a specific focus on events thought to be connected with this nurturing of children's inventiveness and originality. 'Teacher encourages divergent thinking' or 'pupil produces unusual idea', and the consequences of these acts, are among categories that might be conceived and used in lesson observation.

Grouping

There is often public debate about the use of what are sometimes called 'formal' and 'informal', or 'traditional' and 'progressive' teaching styles. Too frequently the discussion is polarised, as if one style is generally preferable to another, or even as if there is complete agreement about what constitutes 'formality' or 'progressiveness'. More accurately the debate is about the suitability of general teaching styles and specific strategies to particular contexts; whether, for example, it would be more effective to give information or elicit it, or whether it would be more appropriate to use whole class, small group or individual teaching for a certain purpose or activity.

When coding classroom interaction it is possible to record at the same time the nature of the grouping, without adding significantly to the burden of the observer. This can be valuable in highlighting such matters as what pupils do under different conditions, or what happens during the transitions from whole class teaching to group work. Suppose a simple category system were being used which recorded whenever the teacher asked a question or gave a reprimand, then by adding the suffix C = Class, G = Group, I = Individual, T = Transition from one type of grouping to another, an important aspect of context would be preserved. If TQ = Teacher asks question, and TR = Teacher reprimands or admonishes, the following could easily be coded:

TQC   Teacher asks question to whole class
TRI   Teacher reprimands individual pupil
TQG   Teacher asks question to group of pupils
TRCT   Teacher reprimands whole class during transition

The use of simple suffixes like this is a useful way of adding valuable context information to a category system without making it over-complex. This will be further discussed below.

Figure 2.3 Teacher counselling individual pupil

Counselling

Not all observations of teaching occur in large classrooms with thirty pupils. Sometimes teachers may be observed during an important part of their day when they are not in the company of the whole class, or when they are talking with individuals. Counselling children about their work, career, behaviour or aspirations is an example of an aspect of teaching that can occur with two or three children or even just one individual pupil. Many aspects of larger group dynamics may occur in this more intimate context, as pupils ask questions, teachers give or solicit information, praise or admonish, but there may be additional elements that are more likely to occur in a one-to-one exchange. A category system for these purposes might note down such matters as when the teacher gives advice and whether the pupil appears to accept or reject it, or whether it is not possible to judge. There are other examples of teacher-pupil interaction away from the classroom – in the playground, library or dining room, perhaps – where certain additional categories may be needed.

Physical environment

When the location of an activity needs to be preserved, for instance, if an individual pupil's movements during the school day are being noted, then it is easy to devise a simple set of categories to note where the activity under scrutiny actually takes place. The following is a simplified example:

L   Laboratory
RC   Reading corner
G   Gymnasium
H   Hall
P   Playground
DR   Dining room

A study of several individual young children might discover which pupils go to the reading corner and which do not. Another observer might focus on the differences in social behaviour in various parts of the school, where and when disruption is most likely to occur, or whether a school's policy on discipline appears to be consistently applied in different locations and contexts.

Pupils

Many category systems concentrate on logging the teacher's behaviour or movements, but others focus specifically on, or take into account, what the pupils do. A good example would be the observations of, say, differences in behaviour between boys and girls, or between children from different groups. An observer studying individual children to see whether the teacher's interactions with boys was similar to, or different from those with girls, could add the suffix B or G to each teacher question, praise, reprimand or whatever to show whether it was addressed to a boy or a girl. It is also possible to code teachers' and pupils' behaviour in an even-handed manner by using a *reciprocal* category system, that is one which has exactly the same categories for both. Thus TQP could be 'Teacher questions pupil', but equally PQT would be 'Pupil questions teacher'. This can lead to some categories that are commonplace and others that are rare, like 'Teacher praises pupil' and 'Pupil praises teacher', but nonetheless it does not weigh down the observer with as many assumptions as some systems.

Theories and ideologies

Just as behaviour modification is rooted firmly in the traditions of behaviourism, so too teachers and observers with particular beliefs and concerns may prefer to use a category system influenced by some theoretical or ideological perspective. The main problem here is that any record of observation can become self-fulfilling, merely confirming the prejudgements of the people concerned. For example, a loaded category like 'Teacher works hard' or 'Girl ill-treated by boy', if not counter-balanced by other different categories, could give a very distorted view of classroom events.

An interesting example occurs in the observations of teachers' questions. Some category systems assume that certain kinds of questions are superior to others, and it is easy to assemble a hierarchy which does precisely that, such as assigning levels to questions which require different degrees of mental effort:

Level 1 Recall of facts
Level 2 Grouping facts
Level 3 Evaluating facts
Level 4 Making inferences from facts

Though it is legitimate to assume that making inferences from facts can represent a greater use of brain power by the learner than merely recalling them, this does not stand up in all circumstances. Suppose you decide to pay a surprise call on friends, hoping to have a chat with them. When you arrive you notice a sign on the door. If you then use the two facts that (a) the house door is locked and (b) the sign on the door says 'Gone fishing' to make the inference that the people you are visiting are not at home, this simple piece of deduction could not be said to operate at three levels higher than recalling the formula of DNA. Some observation schedules have been influenced by such perspectives as the theories of child development of Jean Piaget (1954), the taxonomy of educational objectives formulated by Benjamin Bloom (1956), the non-directive client-centred philosophy of Carl Rogers (1970) and the views of John Dewey (1916).

Non-verbal categories

Many of the published category systems focus exclusively on speech, but some look at non-verbal aspects such as movement, gesture or facial expression. It is possible to use squared paper, for example, to track a teacher's or pupil's movements during lessons. This might be of interest in an open plan school if the teacher and observer wanted to know how frequently the different parts of the school, like the reading area, or the number corner, were actually visited. Observers looking at gesture and facial expression might use categories such as 'Teacher indicates', 'Pupil raises hand', 'Teacher smiles' or 'Pupil appears puzzled'. Some of these categories clearly require more of a degree of subjective judgement.

In order to record posture and positioning, Hall (1963), an anthropologist, used iconic symbols to note where people sat or stood in relationship to each other.

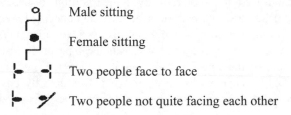

Male sitting

Female sitting

Two people face to face

Two people not quite facing each other

Time sampling

One of the decisions that observers have to make is how often to record a category. There are several choices available, and the following are among the most common.

Figure 2.4 Non-verbal aspects of communication

Unit sampling

A particular time unit is chosen, it may be as short as three or four seconds, or as long as five minutes or more. The main argument for a very short period of time is that it allows for rapidly changing events to be recorded in full, but on the other hand it can be quite tiring for the observer to tally every few seconds, especially if the schedule is long and complex. When longer periods of a minute or more are used, several events can take place even within a short period of time. There are two common conventions which are used in these circumstances. The first is to note down *every single time* something happens, so that if a teacher asks ten questions in the two minute (or whatever) time segment, all ten are recorded. The second convention is to tick each category *once only* during the period under review, so the teacher asking one, two or twenty questions would produce just a single tick in the 'Teacher asks questions' box. The arguments for and against each of these conventions are finely balanced. Trying to record every instance of an event is exhausting, but does produce a fuller record, whereas coding each event once gives the essential flavour of what happened in the lesson, and is manageable by the observer, but can distort the balance of events by suggesting that they were all equivalent.

Static sampling

Some observers build up a series of snapshots of a lesson, a little bit like a time-lapse series of photographs. This means that they code what is happening at some regular interval, perhaps at the end of every minute. Suppose the observer were studying four individual children, two boys and two girls, then at the end of each period there would be a record of exactly where each child was and the nature of its activity at precisely that moment. The advantages of this kind of sampling are that it allows twenty or thirty such snapshots to be collected in quite a short time, preserves the sequence of events, and permits analysis that is not too time-consuming. The major disadvantage is that significant developments can occur between sampling, especially if the time period is a long one.

Natural sampling

Given the problems of choosing a fixed time period in advance, some observers prefer to respond to natural units in which something interesting occurs. Thus if the teacher begins the lesson with a three minute explanation of what is going to happen in that lesson, goes on to twenty minutes of practical work, brings the whole class together again for four minutes to check out what they have learned, and finally asks the pupils to clear away for two minutes before moving on to another activity, then those would be the observer's sampling units, as they reflect the actual periods of time in which specific activities took place.

Other quantitative methods

There are other ways in which classroom observation can be quantified. Certain of these are quite controversial, and indeed seen as threatening by some teachers, so that they are not always widely used. They include quality grading, rank ordering, time lines and target pupils.

Quality grading

Some observers give a single grade of teaching quality as a result of watching lessons. For many years in teacher training there was a widespread use of a five or three point scale for rating the quality of teaching seen during teaching practice. The three point scale was often 'Distinction', 'Pass' and 'Fail', whereas the five point scale was based on the literal grades A B C D E, sometimes with plus and minus signs attached, and C+ became the sort of mark that would be awarded to some honest plodder who was conscientious but not too stimulating. Veteran appraisers would confidently pronounce 'C minus written all over him' or 'B plus, though I could even be persuaded to go as far as A minus if you press me' at meetings of examiners. External inspectors of schools have often used similar three, five or seven point gradings of quality when they observe teaching.

Quality gradings are usually used by observers who see many people teaching, like inspectors and teacher trainers, and their use has declined and risen over a period of decades, as the use of quality grading comes in or out of fashion. The two categories Pass and Fail cannot be avoided by those who have to decide whether trainees should be given qualified teacher status or be allowed to proceed beyond any probationary period.

One of the reasons for the decline of single grades for quality was that teaching became recognised as a multi- rather than unidimensional activity, and it was thought that giving a single grade of 5 out of 10, or B(+) for several diverse activities, might be less effective than drawing up a descriptive profile under various headings such as 'Preparation and planning', 'Class management', 'Relationships' or 'Assessment of children's work'. Nonetheless, numerical or literal gradings of the kind described above are still in use, and those employing them need to make sure they know what their grades mean and what the impact of awarding them may be. It is more common nowadays for grades to have criteria attached, as described above in the section on behaviourally anchored rating scales.

Rank ordering

It is extremely uncommon for teachers to be rank-ordered as a result of classroom observation. Most observations are for specific purposes, such as teacher training, appraisal or research, so there is very little need to assemble a list of the best teacher seen, the second best and so on. However, there are some occasions when rank ordering may take place. It may happen when merit or bonus payments are assigned to some teachers, but not others, on the basis of perceived competence in the classroom; or when certain teachers have to be selected to proceed to some higher salary scale, as they are thought to be especially skilled. Rank ordering does take place when the number of merit payments available has not been determined in advance, so that a cut-off point can be decided once the availability of bonus payments is known.

Rank ordering is almost always contentious, whether the rankings are secret or public, and all the same strictures apply that are cited for single quality grading: that teaching is not unidimensional, that the judgement is highly subjective, that there are many criteria that can be applied, and that it is difficult to say whether a conscientious introvert should be ranked higher than an extravert who appears more spectacular when observed. The danger in both quality grading and rank ordering in classroom observation is that too much emphasis is placed on viewable performance and that morale suffers when the outcomes are known. Whether to use this approach in classroom observation at all is a decision that should be weighed carefully, as it is too sensitive a matter to be undertaken lightly, and that is why it has been undertaken infrequently, compared with other quantitative approaches.

Time lines

Sometimes the observer wishes to preserve some simple information, such as how long a particular activity lasted. One way of doing this economically is to draw a line across the page representing the length of time spent on the aspect of the lesson being studied, using graph paper if necessary. An observer might, for example, be watching a foreign language lesson, and wish to know whether the teacher was talking, or a pupil, or no one, in which case the time line might look like this:

teacher talks   _____   _____   _____
pupil talks   _____   _____   _____
no one talks   _____

Target pupils

If observers wish to study individual pupils using a quantitative approach, whether this is in the form of time lines or other forms of record, it is often difficult to tag the movements or contributions of thirty different individuals who may, during a day, be engaged in hundreds of interactions with their teachers or fellow pupils. One common way round this difficulty is to choose a sub-group and concentrate on observing these alone. Frequently the observer will select a group of six pupils, three boys and three girls, chosen from high, medium and low abilities, hoping that these will be representative of the overall patterns observed in the class. Each child may be observed in turn, or alternatively a suffix may be added to any category system to show which child was involved in the particular event. Thus if the observer wanted to know about the distribution of questions to different children, or the monitoring and assessment of their work, the letters a, b, c, d, e and f could be attached to show who was involved at the time.

Samples other than six can be chosen, as can criteria other than ability or sex. An observer in a multicultural school might concentrate on perhaps four pairs of pupils from Afro-Caribbean, Asian, British and Hispanic backgrounds. In the Leverhulme Primary Improvement Project (Wragg et al., 1998) we wanted to know how different children fared in terms of their progress in reading over a whole school year. We selected three boys and three girls in each of the thirty-five classes we observed. This gave us a set of 210 individual profiles, evenly spread across boys and girls and high, medium and low ability pupils. We also asked teachers, half way through the year, to choose another two pupils who seemed to be making particularly good progress, thus giving us eight target children in each class.

Using a systematic approach

It is worthwhile learning how to use one or two category systems that have been employed over the years, simply to see how they work in practice, even if you do not intend to apply the actual schedule yourself, as it helps you get the feel of coding events in a systematic way. The following section contains details about two contrasting systems, the Flanders Interaction Analysis Category System

(FIAC) and the Exeter Primary Class Management Schedule, referred to from now on simply as the 'Exeter schedule'. The difference between an observation system that notes categories every time they occur and one that tallies each category once only, irrespective of how often the event happens, is sometimes signalled in the name used. The former is often referred to as a *category system*, the latter as a *sign system*. The difference, in simplified form, is shown below. The *category system* has recorded all instances that took place in ten minutes. The *sign system* only tallies once in each of five two minute segments. Both, therefore, represent ten minutes of classroom time. The thicker line separating the first three lesson segments from the next two in the *sign system* is there to help observers remember which segment they are recording in, as it can easily become confusing when using a long or elaborate schedule.

Category system

1	*Teacher asks questions*	/ / / / / / / / / / / / / /	14
2	*Teacher gives command*	/ / /	3
3	*Teacher gives praise*	/ / / / / / / /	8
4	*Teacher uses criticism*	/ /	2

Sign system

1	*Teacher asks question*	/	/	/		/	/
2	*Teacher gives command*	/		/			
3	*Teacher gives praise*	/	/	/		/	/
4	*Teacher uses criticism*	/					/

There are advantages and disadvantages of each type of system. The category system shows all interactions, but the sign system allows the observer to preserve something of the flavour of each lesson segment. In the section below there is an example of each of these types. The category system, FIAC, involves coding what is happening every three seconds, whereas the Exeter schedule for studying the management of pupil behaviour in the primary school is a sign system which requires the observer to tally once only when something occurs in each of five consecutive one and a half minute segments of lesson time.

Flanders Interaction Analysis Categories (FIAC)

The work of Ned Flanders (1970), who analysed the verbal interaction between teachers and pupils, was strongly influenced by the positivist tradition in which Withall (1949) and others worked. Indeed, Flanders's ten category system FIAC is quite close in concept to Withall's four 'learner-centred' and three 'teacher-centred' categories described in Chapter 1, and the ideology pervading it was strongly influenced by interest in democracy in the classroom in the United States after the Second World War. The ten categories are as given below; there is no scale implied by the actual numbers 1 to 10, as they are simply the numbers of each category.

1 *Accepts feeling*: accepts and clarifies the feeling tone of the pupils in a non-threatening manner. Feelings may be positive or negative. Predicting and recalling feelings are included.

2 *Praises or encourages*: praises or encourages pupil action or behaviour, jokes that release tension, not at the expense of another individual, nodding head or saying 'uh uh' or 'go on' are included.

3 *Accepts or uses ideas of student*: clarifying, building or developing ideas or suggestions by a pupil. As teacher brings more of his or her own ideas into play, shift to category 5.

4 *Asks question*: asking a question about content or procedure with the intent that a pupil should answer.

5 *Lectures:* giving facts or opinions about content or procedure; expressing own ideas; asking rhetorical questions.

6 *Gives directions*: directions, commands or orders with which a pupil is expected to comply.

7 *Criticises or justifies authority*: statements, intended to change pupil behaviour from non-acceptable to acceptable pattern, bawling someone out; stating why the teacher is doing what he or she is doing, extreme self-reference.

8 *Student talk-response*: talk by pupils in response to teacher. Teacher initiates the contact or solicits pupil statement.

9 *Student talk-initiation*: talk by pupils, which they initiate. If 'calling on' pupils is only to indicate who may talk next, observer must decide whether pupil wanted to talk. If pupil did, use this category.

10 *Silence or confusion*: pauses, short periods of silence and periods of confusion in which communication cannot be understood by the observer.

The reason that FIAC is described here is not because it is the best system, indeed there have been many refinements and modifications of it, but rather because it is an example of a simple category system that has been widely used in its original or modified form in teacher training, lesson analysis and research. It illustrates very well the strengths and weaknesses of quantitative approaches. The FIAC system is not difficult to learn or apply, though tallying every three seconds becomes quite demanding and an observer can become fatigued after about half an hour, so it is advisable to observe for twenty to thirty minutes at a time, with a gap in between. Observers learn to use the ten categories and then check the level of agreement between each other, a procedure described more fully in Chapter 5.

Using FIAC in the classroom involves the following steps:

1 The observer has a data recording sheet (see p. 38) with twenty squares available for each minute of time. Every three seconds the category number

is recorded (e.g. 4 for a teacher question, 8 for a pupil reply) which best describes what is taking place.

2 The observer records *across* the record sheet so that each line represents one minute of classroom time.

3 Separate 'episodes', such as 'setting up', 'monitoring pupil work' or 'summary', can be identified in the margin, so that it is clear later what kind of interaction occurred during various kinds of activities.

4 A stopwatch, the second hand of a wristwatch, or even a specially designed pocket timer which gives a bleep to an earpiece, can be used to remind the observer to record a category every three seconds.

Let us take a simple exchange which will show how the system works in practice:

		Category tallied
Teacher:	Look at the list of cities on the blackboard.	6 (*command*)
	Which do you think is the one nearest here?	4 (*question*)
	(*three second pause*)	10 (*silence*)
Pupil:	It's either Bristol or Birmingham.	8 (*solicited pupil talk*)

The sequence recorded on the data sheet could, therefore, be 6–4–10–8.

It is worth looking at some of the Flanders categories in a little more detail, as the strengths and weaknesses of such systems soon become apparent.

Category 1

Accepting or clarifying feelings is a relatively infrequent category that occurs more often in lessons like English than science, more often with younger pupils than older.

Category 2

One weakness of the FIAC system is that it does not distinguish between cursory praise ('Good', 'Fine', 'Right') which may be as regular and frequent as raindrops, and enthusiastic or effusive praise, such as, 'That's a really good answer, Paul, well done'. Flanders suggests ignoring what he calls 'merely verbal habits' like 'OK' or a cursory 'Right' or 'Yes', and the same would apply to category 3.

Category 3

Accepting and clarifying pupils' ideas is also relatively infrequent, though more common than category 1. Some teachers use it extensively, however, to weave children's answers into the lesson: 'Now, Sally told us that magnets pick things up, and John said that they didn't attract all metals, so can anyone tell me what exactly magnets do pick up?' This would be a good example of the sequence 3–4, acceptance of pupils' ideas, followed by one or more questions.

FIAC DATA SHEET

School _____   Teacher   _____

Class   _____   Subject/topic _____

Date   _____   Observer   _____

TALLY ACROSS

01																			
02																			
03																			
04																			
05																			
06																			
07																			
08																			
09																			
10																			
11																			
12																			
13																			
14																			
15																			
16																			
17																			
18																			
19																			
20																			
21																			
22																			
23																			
24																			
25																			
26																			
27																			
28																			
29																			
30																			

Category 4

Many other schedules which have built on FIAC have created a set of different categories of question, such as:

4a Question involving recall of factual data
4b Question requiring pupil to group or classify information
4c Question involving evaluation
4d Question involving pupils' imagination

The observer also has to remember to code questions which are really commands, like 'Andrea, would you please hand these papers out?' as category 6, not category 4, for even though the command is expressed in question form, it is really an order with which the pupil is expected to comply. As with all category systems the observers using them must clarify first what conventions they will employ, and then stick to them.

Category 5

One weakness of FIAC is that it does not make any distinctions between the many kinds of information that can be given. For example, all the following would simply be coded as category 5, despite their immense differences:

'An orbiting body possesses angular momentum'
'Ich heisse Herr Splutzenheimer'
'Insects have seven legs'

Other category systems often distinguish between information that is factually correct or incorrect, based on opinions or facts, or which incorporates different levels or types of thinking.

Category 6

Commands are rare in some lessons, but frequent in others, especially in subjects like physical education lessons where, in certain teaching modes, teachers may be very directive. Questions that are disguised commands, 'Would you please ...', are coded as 6, rather than 4.

Category 7

The use of criticism, like that of praise, category 2, varies considerably among teachers. Some observers attach a pupil code number to identify to whom the praise or criticism is addressed, so that 7c would be criticism addressed to pupil C and 2f would be praise given to pupil F. This then allows a profile of the targets of praise and criticism to be assembled. If six target pupils were observed, three boys and three girls, then the resulting profiles of praise and criticism might appear as follows:

	Praise (category 2)	Criticism (category 7)
Alison	11	0
June	2	1
Tracy	5	1
Alan	8	0
Paul	1	5
Simon	3	2

Examples of disguised criticism need to be looked for, especially if the tone of voice emphasises the message. The statement: 'That's a wonderful answer, the mark of a true genius' would be praise (2) if genuine, but criticism (7) if intended as a sarcastic reply to an incorrect answer.

Categories 8 and 9

Many other category systems have an extensive range of possibilities for pupil talk, but FIAC only offers two. The observer needs to look out for a shift from 8 to 9 when the pupil goes beyond the immediate solicited reply:

Teacher:	What was the weather like?	(4)
Pupil	It was pretty bad.	(8)
	But I don't think the weather matters when you're on holiday.	(9)

Category 10

This catch-all category is one of the weakest features of FIAC, which was not really designed either for detailed analysis of pupil talk or for non-verbal aspects of classroom interaction. Many other systems subdivide this category into 'noise', 'confusion', 'complete silence' or whatever else seems appropriate, sometimes using subscripts like 10a, 10b, 10c, 10d and so on.

The following exchange shows how FIAC would be used to code the events that occur. The categories are shown in parentheses after each statement.

Teacher:	So can anyone give me an example of an insect? Richard?	(4)
Pupil 1:	I know, a spider.	(8)
Pupil 2:	A spider's not an insect.	(9)
Teacher:	Good, that's quite right Jacky. Er ...	(2)
	(*Teacher distracted*)	(10)
Teacher:	It's not an insect, because it's got the wrong number of legs.	(5)
	It should have six legs, not eight.	(5)
Pupil 3:	And it's got three parts to its body.	(9)
Teacher:	That's right, Andrew, its body is in three parts,	(3)
	and the middle bit has quite a hard name – the thorax.	(5)

The sequence of exchanges has ten entries into the data sheet and lasts about half a minute. The observer's list of tallies would look like this:

01	4	8	9	2	10	5	5	9	3	5								
02																		

Ned Flanders devised a neat two-dimensional display for FIAC data which preserves the sequence of events and shows where the action is. It consists of a matrix, ten by ten, giving a hundred little squares, or 'cells'. Each pair of events is tallied in one of the cells, so that the sequence *question – answer – praise,* which is coded 4 – 8 – 2, is entered according to the following procedures. The first pair is *question* (4) followed by *solicited answer* (8), so a tick is put into the 4-8 cell (counting *down* 4, *across* 8). But the pupil's answer is also the first event of the next pair, *solicited answer* (8) followed by *praise* (2), so the next tally is entered into the 8-2 cell (*down* 8, *across* 2). The full thirty second sequence of ten tallies recorded above in the lesson on the characteristics of insects, $4 - 8 - 9 - 2 - 10 - 5 - 5 - 9 - 3 - 5$, would look like the illustration when entered in the 10×10 FIAC matrix.

	1	2	3	4	5	6	7	8	9	10
1										
2										/
3					/					
4								/		
5					/				/	
6										
7										
8										
9		/	/							
10					/					

   The display of classroom interaction in this form not only shows how much of the lesson was talk by pupils or teacher, but also reveals the nature of the talk. For example, a programmed learning format consisting of *information – question – answer – praise – next piece of information, etc.* would produce sequences like $5 - 4 - 8 - 2 - 5 - 4 - 8 - 2 - 5$, *etc.*, producing a build-up of tallies in the 5-4, 4-8, 8-2 and 2-5 cells. The 8-7 and 9-7 cells record pupil contributions which resulted in teacher criticism, so rows 8 and 9 show how the teacher responded, perhaps with praise (8-2, 9-2), acceptance or clarification (8-3, 9-3), an immediate question (8-4, 9-4) or further information (8-5, 9-5). A great deal of other information is also revealed, but much is also lost with such reductions, so care must be exercised, as there are no omnipurpose 'good' or 'bad' patterns.

ACTIVITY 4

Analyse the short extracts below using the FIAC system. The text has been split up into short sections, so enter a tally at the end of each line. As a reminder here is a short-hand version of the categories:

Teacher talk

1   accepts feelings
2   praise
3   accepts ideas
4   question
5   lecture
6   command
7   criticism

Pupil talk

8   solicited
9   unsolicited
10 silence, etc

Real classroom interaction is craggy, rather than clear cut and unambiguous, so not every statement lasts exactly three seconds. Flanders recommends that the *predominant* activity should be recorded if two events happen in the same three second segment, but he also suggests that both might be recorded where they appear to be of roughly equal prominence, such as a short answer and brief praise. This illustrates the difficulty of being precise, and underlines once more the need for caution with quantitative methods.

Extract 1   *Category*

Teacher: What happens to your colour (*blue*) when you add yellow to it?
Pupil 1:   It goes dark green.
Teacher: How many colours have you got here?
             They're all green, but they're different, aren't they?
Pupil 2:   I've got two greens now.
Teacher: So you have. What did you add to it? Blue or white?
             What happens when you add white to it?
Pupil 2:   Light.
Teacher: It's a light green, that's right.
             (*To another pupil*) That's a super green, how did you make that one?

Pupil 3:	Yellow and dark green.
Teacher:	That's like a spring green, isn't it, very bright ... Lovely ...
	Dip your brush in there, make it clean and then take some more powder.
	Wipe it on the side, then pick up more powder.

Extract 2   *Category*

Pupil 1:	Miss, Brian's taken my ruler.
Teacher:	Brian, have you taken Alan's ruler?
Pupil 2:	He took my pen first, miss.
	I just took his ruler to get my pen back, he started it.
Pupil 1:	No I didn't, you liar.
Teacher:	Stop it, both of you.
	I'm fed up of your stupid behaviour,
	so will you go over there and sit by Debbie
	and Alan you can sit next to my desk.
	(*six seconds of pupils moving*)
	Now, let's get back to our topic.
	Who can tell me something else about levers?

Figure 2.5 Accepting a pupil's idea

Extract 3		Category
Teacher:	Is a woodlouse an insect?	
Pupil 1:	Yes.	
Teacher:	Does it look like an insect?	
Pupil 1:	Sort of.	
Teacher:	What about its three body parts?	
	Can you find the head, thorax and abdomen?	
Pupil 1:	I can't find the thorax and abdomen.	
Pupil 2:	It looks like it's got lots of little body parts.	
Teacher:	Ah! How many legs has it got?	
Pupil 2:	More than six.	
Teacher:	More than six, and lots of body parts.	
	Is it an insect?	
Pupil 1:	It can't be.	

You probably felt some occasional uncertainty about the use of category 2 or 3, for example when the teacher says 'Lovely', leaving the observer uncertain whether to record it as praise, which it is, or acceptance of a pupil's idea, which it also is. Another difficulty may have been the handling of repetition of answers, which may be seen as category 3 if the idea is genuinely accepted, but again FIAC does not distinguish clearly between mechanical repetition of what has just been said and genuine acceptance, enhancement or clarification. Perhaps in Extract 3 you were uncertain when to use command (6) and criticism (7).

Nonetheless, despite the problems, trained observers will agree with each other about category assignment over 80–90 per cent of events. That still, however, leaves some 15 per cent or so of disagreement, and it is often over the assignment of a 2 or a 3, an 8 or a 9, that observers disagree. The Flanders system is easiest to use during whole class teaching or when the interactions are public. It is more difficult, though not impossible to apply, when the teacher is working with individuals or small groups, and it is usual to code the teacher's interactions with the individuals concerned, a process greatly helped if a radio microphone is available, or if the observer can stay fairly near the teacher without being too intrusive.

The Exeter schedule

The schedule devised at Exeter University during the Leverhulme Primary Project for observing how teachers manage pupils' behaviour (Wragg 1993a) is an example of a sign system. There are two parts to it: the first deals with pupils' misbehaviour and how the teacher does or does not respond to it, the second consists of an individual pupil study which allows the observer to build up a profile of how involved in the task children appear to be, and whether or not they misbehave.

The full schedule is too long to reproduce in its entirety, so an abbreviated version is given below. It consists of a set of categories which the observer ticks at the end of each one and a half minute period. Once trained, observers need about thirty to forty seconds to complete the checking of categories for that segment. The blocks of segments are in sets of five with a double line splitting the first three segments from the other two. The observer tallies *down* the page. A completed first segment on a selection of categories (the schedule below is abbreviated for convenience) would look like this:

Type of misbehaviour

Noisy or illicit talk	/					
Inappropriate movement	/					
Inappropriate use of materials						
Damage to materials/equipment						
Taking something without permission	/					
Physical aggression to another pupil						
Defiance of teacher	/					
Refusal to move						

This represents a lesson segment in which there was noisy or illicit chatter, inappropriate movement, someone took something from another pupil without permission, and then defied the teacher.

Sometimes the observer will tick only one category in a section during each segment of the lesson. For example, the first part of the schedule, which records the type of activity, shows how this works. The observer has to decide the predominant type of activity during the segment, which might have been pupil–teacher interaction, or the pupils might have worked alone or in groups with the teacher monitoring. In each one and a half minute segment only one choice is ticked. The illustration shows the box ticked in each of five successive lesson segments.

Activity

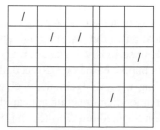

Teacher solo	/					
Teacher–pupil interaction		/	/			
Pupils working, teacher monitoring					/	
Pupils working, teacher not monitoring						
Transition without movement				/		
Transition with movement						

In the first segment the teacher was talking to the whole class, in the second and third there was teacher-pupil interaction, in the fourth segment a changeover took place and the children began to work in their groups, so 'transition without movement' is recorded, and in the fifth segment the teacher walked round monitoring pupils' work.

Other sections of the Exeter schedule cover pupil misbehaviour, and record whether there were no pupils misbehaving, one pupil only, two to four pupils, or five or more. If misbehaviour does occur, then the observer goes on to code teacher response, whether it was to the whole class, a small group, or an individual, and whether it occurred before or after escalation. Next there is a set of categories describing the teacher's response, including the following.

Teacher's response

Order to cease

Pupil named

Reprimand

Involve pupils in work

Proximity (going over to pupils)

Touch

Humour

Praise/encouragement

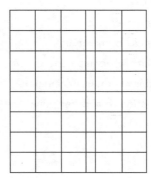

The subsequent part of the schedule records pupil responses, whether they fell silent, altercated or protested, whether the misbehaviour ceased, lessened, remained the same, or increased. The observer ticks each category when it occurs, sometimes checking several, sometimes choosing one from a set of options. After several lesson segments have been observed in this way, the observer can build up a profile of the lesson, or of several lessons.

The first section of the Exeter schedule uses a checklist approach to record classroom events. In order to supplement this picture with information about individual children, therefore, the second part of the schedule requires the observer to study every single pupil in the class one by one. For this exercise a different kind of data sheet is required, with spaces for each individual child. The observer must concentrate on one pupil for 20 seconds before moving on to the next child and eventually covering every pupil in the class this way. In each case the observer makes two decisions: whether the pupil is high, medium or low, in terms of application to the task in hand, and whether the child is not misbehaving, or is mildly or seriously deviant during the period of observation. Below is a data sheet for six pupils, based on a 20 second observation period. In this case the criteria for deciding the involvement level would be the number of seconds during the observation that the child appeared to be engaged in the task: 'low' would be 0 to 6 seconds, 'medium' 7 to 13, and 'high' 14 to 20 seconds. Misbehaviour would be coded either as 'none', or as 'mild' if it included minor matters such as noisy or illicit chatter, and 'serious' if physical aggression, threat to the teacher or damage to property were noted. All these conventions have to be agreed in advance by the observers.

	Involvement level			Deviancy level		
Pupil	low	medium	high	none	mild	serious
01	/			/		
02			/	/		
03		/			/	
04		/		/		
05			/	/		
06	/					/

This schedule would show that pupil 1 did not appear to be involved in the task, but was not misbehaving, whereas pupil 6 was not involved in his work, but was engaging in more serious misbehaviour. Although highly engaged pupils do not usually misbehave, it is possible to see almost any combination in the two parts of the observation schedule. The observer can study each individual child in the class

Figure 2.6 Pupil reflecting, or day-dreaming?

several times in rotation and build up a profile of the behaviour and application of both the individual and the whole class. Frequently the decision about involvement or deviancy is self-evident, but there are particular problems when pupils are not misbehaving but simply sitting quietly. They might be reflecting on their work or day-dreaming, it is sometimes impossible to tell with any precision. That is why such quantitative measures as are described in this chapter are useful, but should be regarded as rough and ready, rather than precise measures, and should certainly be related to other kinds of information when it comes to interpretation and analysis. Later chapters in this book will show how quantitative and qualitative methods can be combined.

To conclude this chapter consider the following activity.

ACTIVITY 5

Read the transcript below and note down some *quantitative* information that might be of interest. At the end of it are a few suggestions.

Teacher:	Can you see anything that attracts you about the Island? Anywhere you'd like to visit, David?
Pupil 1:	Castle Point.
Teacher:	Why would you like to go there?
Pupil 1:	It's exciting.
Teacher:	Yes, it's exciting. Have you found anywhere you'd like to go, Emma?
Pupil 2:	I think ...
Teacher:	No, it's Emma's turn. I'd like to hear what Emma has to say.
Pupil 3:	Eastern Moors. There's a creature ... it's ... it's ...
Teacher:	There's something up there that Emma's found. What has she found coming out of the sea?
Pupil 4:	A monster.
Teacher:	Yes, it could be. What's coming out of his hand?
Pupil 2:	Lightning.
Teacher:	What else has he got coming out of him?
Pupil 2:	Rain.
Teacher:	Rain and thunder, so it's almost as if he's in control of the ...?
Pupil 2:	Weather.
Teacher:	The weather, yes, I think so ... What would be a good word to describe Darkling Forest?
Pupil 2:	Spooky and creepy.

> *Teacher:*   Better than 'spooky and creepy'?
> *Pupil 1:*   Strange and weird.
> *Teacher:*   Yes, strange and weird.
>   How about a word beginning with two e's?
>   Do you know it?
> *Pupil 1:*   Eerie.
> *Teacher:*   Yes. What does 'eerie' mean?
> *Pupil 1:*   Scary.

Using FIAC this sequence might come out as $4 - 4 - 8 - 4 - 8 - 3 - 4 - 9$ (different pupil answers) $- 7$ ('No, it's Emma's turn' is a reprimand) $- 8 - 3 - 4 - 8 - 3$ (though 'it could be' is a little grudging) $- 4 - 8 - 4 - 8 - 3$ (teacher accepts 'rain' and enhances it) $- 4 - 8 - 3 - 4 - 8 - 4$ (not 3, as the teacher asks for something better) $- 8 - 3 - 4 - 4 - 8 - 4$ (possibly with an extra '3' thrown in, as the teacher accepts the word offered) $- 8$. In addition to this kind of analysis, however, there are many other quantitative statements that could be made about the exchange, if one had all the necessary information, such as:

Pupils participating	4
Teacher's questions	12
Open questions	7 (approximately)
Closed questions	5 (approximately)
Statements of approval	5
Statements of disapproval	2
Reprimands	1
Length of episode	68 seconds
Total number of words uttered	164
Words spoken by teacher	138
Words spoken by pupils	26
Percentage teacher talk	84 per cent
Percentage pupil talk	16 per cent
Length of pauses	19 seconds
Length of talk	49 seconds
Number of teacher utterances	12
Number of pupil utterances	12
Percentage of talk	72 per cent
Percentage of non-talk (pauses etc.)	28 per cent
Average length of each teacher utterance	11.5 words
Average length of each pupil utterance	2.17 words
Average length of each pause between teacher and pupil talk	0.83 seconds

Number of key concepts   4
      1 Where to visit
      2 Why place attracts
      3 The nature of the creature
      4 The nature of the forest

There are, therefore, numerous ways in which observers can quantify what happens in the classroom, but there are also very important qualitative aspects of the lesson extract above, like gesture, factual accuracy, voice, body language, classroom climate, use of learning aids, understandings, misunderstandings, interpretations, meanings, inferences and numerous others. It is to these that we shall now turn in Chapter 3.

The use of qualitative methods

There are thousands of published and unpublished schedules for studying what happens in the classroom, as has been described in Chapter 2 on quantitative methodology, but qualitative methods are just as many and varied. There are numerous approaches which try to probe beneath the surface of events, to elicit the meanings, sometimes deeply buried, the interpretations and explanations, significance and impact of classroom life. Trying to explain the meaning of a particular incident in a classroom to an intelligent Martian would not be straight-forward, as explanations are sometimes easiest when a great deal can be taken for granted, or when there is a background of shared assumptions.

There is, however, a serious danger with the taken-for-granted. Explanations are first of all intensely subjective. Second, the individual subjectivity of a collection of people who communicate frequently can readily become compounded, with judgement and assertion repeated and reinforced by others to the point where they become reified, accepted as 'true', beyond reproof. When a football referee fails to give a penalty kick to the home team, the immediate reaction of 30,000 supporters is to scream abuse, question his eyesight and even his parentage, and convince themselves that he is at best biased, at worst a complete villain, probably bribed by the opposition. For some people the experience of seeing the video replay, and watching in slow motion the unambiguous evidence that the referee was actually correct in his decision, will make little difference. We often interpret events as we wish to see them, not as they are. There can be several filters along the route, as information about an event speeds towards the human brain. Good qualitative analysis of classroom behaviour involves rigorous scrutiny of these barriers to accurate perception.

I once read a dissertation based on several observations of primary classes. Throughout the whole of the lengthy account the writer used the term 'good primary practice', over and over again, without once attempting to define what it was. There was an assumption that the whole community must surely share her view of what was desirable and effective, and there was no need for critical analysis. Yet Ronald King (1978) in his study of infant classrooms *All Things Bright and Beautiful?* spent 600 hours observing lessons and, while he saw a number of features common to more than one classroom, did not label these 'good primary practice'. Indeed, terms like 'good' and 'effective', though uttered regularly in everyday conversation, have to be used with care. Classroom observers seen to have a single fixed stereotype of what is 'good' may be met with scorn or contempt, if their views are out of harmony with those of the teacher being observed, or with fear and apprehension if they are thought to be in a position of power and influence.

Observers who use qualitative methods are of many kinds. Most informal and semi-formal observations of lessons, such as teachers sitting in on each other's classes, the supervision of student teachers, visitors to schools who have come to 'watch some teaching', tend to adopt qualitative rather than quantitative approaches. Many observers simply form impressions about the generalities of classroom life: whether pupils appear to be busy; if the teacher seems to know the subject or topic; if the teacher is in charge; whether the children are behaving well or badly; what is displayed on classroom walls. These perceptions are simply filtered, absorbed, occasionally discussed, sometimes written down, depending on the circumstances. In more formal settings an appraiser might use a qualitative approach, perhaps making notes and then discussing these with the teacher being appraised. Another possibility is that a trainee teacher or a researcher will be observing a lesson with a specific brief, and therefore be compiling notes for a report or action project.

The influences on this tradition are quite different from those described in Chapter 2. Some observers, like Sara Delamont (1976) who used a mixture of methods, are influenced by George Mead, the American philosopher and social psychologist, who taught at Chicago University in the early part of the twentieth century. Mead advocated the study of the symbols that are part of interaction between people, that is their language, appearance and gesture. This school of thought is sometimes called 'symbolic interactionism', and even those who have not read the seminal texts, like Mead's *Mind, Self and Society* (1934), are often, albeit unwittingly or at second hand, following some of its precepts. *Participant observation*, whereby the observer joins in activities and talks to the other people involved, is a role frequently played not only by researchers studying an institution as outsiders, but also by teachers or other insiders looking at the world in which they work.

By contrast, other classroom observers might be influenced by a particular philosophy or school of thought. Those taking a Marxist perspective, for example, like Sharp and Green (1975) who looked at an infants' school in a working-class area, will see the classroom as part of a wider social context. Their conclusion that teachers act as agents of social control on behalf of a capitalist society will, to some extent, be predetermined by their initial perspective, just as was that of the teacher who sought to confirm her notion of 'good primary practice'. A bell ringing at the end of a lesson may be seen as the normal signal to move on to the next subject by a secondary teacher observing a colleague, but a Marxist observer may regard it as an illustration of the way in which schools prepare working-class pupils for obedience to orders in the factory production line. No doubt a bell manufacturer would be concentrating on the penetration of its sound.

Figure 3.1 The interview after the observation

In qualitative analysis it is not a prerequisite that the observer should be a central part of the school. Although some observers wish to become, or already are enmeshed in classroom life, others working in a similar tradition try to keep their distance. The study by King (1978) of infant school classrooms was a *non-participant* observation. He was strongly influenced by the German sociologist Max Weber (1947), whose action theory put forward the notion that the subjective meanings attached to events by individuals are inseparable from social structure. This view requires the classroom observer to understand and explain how teachers act, usually by first observing and then interviewing. Teaching is such a rapidly moving set of activities, that the way in which teachers, and for that matter pupils, see and interpret what happens, is often neglected. Observations and interviews allow the taken-for-granted to be explored in greater detail.

In a later account of what he actually did, King describes how this approach to studying the events he observed in infant schools actually worked in practice. As he constantly had to find a safe refuge where he could write up his field notes, away from the eyes of those he was studying, he called his account *The Man in the Wendy House*. He collected several notebooks of jottings about what happened in the lessons he observed, but did not wish to become part of the teaching staff, though he was an experienced secondary school teacher, a stance which sometimes caused difficulties, especially with young pupils' natural tendency to want to talk to anyone visiting the classroom:

I lacked the professional competences. I was too old to fit either the student teacher category ... or become an 'honorary pupil'. ... In my relationship with teachers I drew upon the social qualities of polite acquaintance between middle class men and women. ... Although I felt I was drawing on the anthropological tradition, I was not concerned with the whole way of life of my subjects, which ethnography usually implies. My interest in the teachers was as teachers. ... I did allow myself to be approached by children to begin with, but I soon found that they treated me as a teacher-surrogate as they did other non-teacher adults, showing pictures, asking me spellings. ... I politely refused requests for help, referring the child to the teacher, and met requests for approval only with smiles. To begin with I kept standing so that physical height maintained social distance. Most importantly I avoided eye contact; if you do not look, you will not be seen. These measures led to my being, for the most part, ignored by the children. ... My intended relationship with the teacher was that of an interested, non-judgemental observer.

(King 1984)

Key concepts and influences

In the literature on qualitative research there are numerous overlapping concepts, some of which have been described above. A researcher engaging in a long-term classroom observation project might be deeply interested in the intellectual basis of and justification for each of these philosophies or concerns. Someone simply observing lessons out of interest, or appraising a fellow teacher's classroom 'performance', on the other hand, may have little interest in what may appear somewhat arcane distinctions between different philosophies and vantage points. Yet even those who do not wish to read extensively about ideologies, philosophies or traditions, will still need to consider certain issues, such as whether they should be a participant or a non-participant observer. If you are observing in an infants' school classroom and a child asks you how to spell a word, you need to decide that you will either give the answer, or, as King (1984) did, refer the child to the teacher. Whether this is done purely on intuition, on the basis of reasoned argument, or under the influence of Weber, is a matter of personal taste.

Bryman (1988) has summarised the main influences on qualitative research as coming under five headings: phenomenology, symbolic interactionism, 'verstehen', naturalism and ethogenics. These are not the only key terms and concepts, but some of their relevance to classroom observation and the issues they raise are summarised below.

Phenomenology

This is one of a number of generic terms used to embrace those people who concentrate on how we interpret our world, the phenomena that surround us. It rejects the quantitative approach described in Chapter 2 on the grounds that this imposes the observer's rational presuppositions on to events in a systematic way, rather than seeing them through the eyes of those being observed. Its beliefs were formulated by the German philosopher Edmund Husserl in the early part of the twentieth century and have been influential on psychologists of the *Gestalt* school, who believe that the whole is greater than the sum of its parts, and on literary figures such as Jean-Paul Sartre.

Various methods of observation and enquiry are used and related traditions, like *ethnomethodology*, the study of how people perceive and make sense of their daily routines, and *symbolic interactionism* (see below), are often subsumed under the broad heading of 'phenomenology'. So far as classroom observation is concerned it will frequently involve making notes about classroom events and interviewing teachers and pupils to see what constructs and interpretations emerge when they talk about the classroom. Often extensive analysis of lesson and interview transcripts is required.

The major benefit of this type of observation is that it does draw on the richness of individuals' personal insights. Its drawback is that, by putting a premium on the subjective, it may simply report personal fantasies, which, important though they may be, are often at variance with actuality. For example, a teacher of 6 year olds may be convinced she has heard almost every child read every day. The reality might be that she hears, on average, a third to a half of the class and that on only two days in a month did she actually hear everyone. Her belief is important, as is the fact that it is verifiably untrue, but her subjective answer is only one part of a larger story, a single snapshot taken through a lens covered by several coloured filters.

Symbolic interactionism

The accounts of symbolic interactionism vary from those that see it as virtually the same as phenomenology, to those that make significant distinctions between the two. Symbolic interactionism has a strong focus on the self, especially on the symbols like language and gesture that we employ when engaging in interaction with others. Our definition and assessment of how our actions will be perceived by others are influential on how we behave. A classroom observer might, therefore, watch lessons and interview teachers and pupils looking at how both believe their actions are interpreted by others. This could include fellow teachers, fellow pupils, or teachers' interpretations of pupils' actions and vice versa.

Verstehen

The German verb *verstehen* simply means 'to understand'. Max Weber, the German sociologist, used the term to describe both the way in which a particular act is understood and the explanation that goes with it. In terms of watching teachers and pupils the observer might seek to recognise not only that the teacher would use a different voice to convey various messages, but also whether that voice was interpreted as signalling impatience, anger, expectation or humour, and what produced these reactions. King (1978) was influenced both by Weber (1947) and by Schutz (1972), who amplified Weber's notion by talking about 'because' motives (retrospective explanation of why something happened) and 'in order to' motives (explaining the intent behind an action). King described a number of voices that infant teachers used to establish and maintain social control. They transmitted such messages as 'now we are going to do something exciting', 'don't be silly', 'I am being very patient with you', 'Oh never mind, let's not have a fuss', a slightly aggrieved, sad voice, and a no-nonsense 'do as I say'.

Naturalism

The study of classrooms in what are often termed 'naturalistic' settings mean that the observer tries to see life as it really is. That rules out experiments, for example, whereby the teacher might be asked to try out a particular method of working to see what the consequences appear to be. The study in the Leverhulme Primary Project (Wragg 1993a) in which teachers were given ten minutes to explain the topic 'insects' to small groups of 8 and 9 year old children would be disregarded, even though it was conducted in teachers' own classrooms, on the grounds that it was done partially under laboratory conditions, rather than being in a 100 per cent natural setting. Quantitative methods are also eschewed completely, as they are seen to be further external intrusions into the natural environment, and therefore likely to distort.

One major criticism of naturalism is that it can appear to take no moral stance and condone whatever happens. For example, in a study of classroom misbehaviour the observer may well appear to be empathising with and finding excuses for pupils who are regarded as the 'deviants'. This is not as controversial as other naturalistic observers looking at violent criminals or drug dealers, where there is an even stronger expectation that the observer will have a personal moral slant towards condemnation rather than empathy. Supporters of naturalism counter this by arguing that there is already too quick a tendency to condemn something like deviance, without looking at how and why it happens. In classroom terms, the 'deviant' may sometimes be the victim; for example, the child who appears to snatch a piece of equipment may have been robbed of his turn on it by others and be desperate to complete his assignment, rather than an embryo criminal. Empathising with the deviant is not exactly new. The nineteenth-century novelist Samuel Butler described an imaginary world in which the sick and unhealthy were punished, and criminals were sent to hospital, in his novel *Erewhon* (1872), though supporters of naturalism might not like the implication that crime is a pathological condition.

Ethogenics

This is an approach to such matters as classroom disruption based on an attempt to study the beliefs which lie beneath sequences of actions. Bryman (1988) described it as follows:

A central feature of the ethogenic approach is the understanding of episodes in social life. 'Episodes' are sequences of interlocking acts by individuals. It is the task of ethogenics to elucidate the underlying structures of such episodes by investigating the meanings actors bring to the constituent acts....The understanding and analysis of such phenomena facilitate the construction of theories about the resources upon which actors draw when acting.

Although ethogenics is another variant of the view that renounces quantitative methodology, its supporters endorse the notion of taking a scientific approach to classroom observation and the understanding of what happens there. It simply rejects positivists' use of quantities to achieve scientific rigour, favouring an alternative form which seeks to *elicit* underlying structure by careful qualitative analysis of sequences of events, rather than impose it by predetermined schedules and other instruments of observation.

All of these approaches and views of the world in general and social interaction in particular have a great deal in common. Even classroom observers who have no intention of reading a single book about the topic would do well to recognise some of the precepts on which they are founded. For example, someone asked to carry out an appraisal of a teacher may feel that the notions described above are irrelevant to the particular task in hand, or even that they are simply abstruse sociological theories. Yet failure to appreciate how the teacher may perceive appraisal, or to understand what may be the wider significance of events in the classroom when the teacher is being observed, would make the appraisal a very superficial and insensitive exercise.

Quality and effectiveness

One of the most frequent outcomes of classroom observation is that the observer is expected to provide, or is asked for, some kind of qualitative assessment of the teacher's competence. Some variation of 'Was that OK?' must be one of the most frequent opening remarks by a student or experienced teacher after a lesson in which an observer has been present. Another common reaction is for the teacher to apologise, even when no apology is sought or indeed regarded as necessary: 'Look, I'm sorry that was a bit boring, but I had to make sure they knew the subject matter'. It is natural reaction after being observed to wonder how the visitor regarded what took place and to seek reassurance or feedback, partly because so few such mirrors are available to teachers.

Judging the quality or effectiveness of what happens in a classroom is not, however, a simple or unidimensional matter. 'Fine', 'OK by me' or 'Carry on the good work' may be the sort of remark that is acceptable in potentially strained circumstances, but serious attempts to watch lessons and then draw out evaluations of quality need some thought. Mostly when we talk about a 'good' teacher, an 'effective' strategy or a 'bad' lesson, we are referring to our own subjective perception. Sometimes we may quote what appears to be external evidence: that several children were seen to be misbehaving; that the teacher made a number of demonstrably inaccurate statements about verifiable factual matters, like classifying a worm as an insect; that the quality of pupils' written work was highly praised by assessors who read it, not just by the teacher; that when the bell went several children carried on working.

The judgement of one observer, both about teaching quality and the evidence for it, might be endorsed by others, but it can also happen that disagreements occur. I once showed a videotape of a student teacher's lesson to thirty-five teacher trainers (Wragg 1974). The marks ranged from D, which at the time was a near failure grade, to B+, a near distinction, and comments varied from condemnation of what some observers saw as lack of structure, to praise for what others regarded as a sensitive response to individual children.

In the nineteenth century, teacher training institutions were called 'normal schools', on the grounds that there was a single approved 'norm' to which teachers were expected to conform. It led Dickens to describe M'Choakumchild in *Hard Times* (1854) as being like 'some one hundred and forty schoolmasters ... turned at the same time in the same factory, like so many pianoforte legs'. From time to time there have been attempts to impose a single teaching style on teachers, but classroom observation studies have shown the importance of the context on what teachers do, and part of the benefit of being observed is that it enables practitioners to decide how to teach more effectively in the light of local circumstances.

Judgement about professional competence nowadays, when a wider range of teaching styles is accepted than might have formerly been the case, is often founded on different criteria. Those who prefer quantitative approaches might look at test scores obtained by children, but others operating to a different agenda might appraise what they see as the quality of learning taking place, without necessarily measuring it. A field like music is an interesting example to consider. If scores on tests alone were considered, then a teacher whose class could all define sonata form, or translate the word *andante*, might be highly esteemed. Longer term aspirations, like whether the teacher is laying the foundations for lifelong enjoyment of music, are less easily measured. Observers can find, therefore, that they are either ignoring such matters, or having to make an intelligent guess about them on the basis of what they see in the classroom.

Criteria which inform judgement about teaching quality or effectiveness can be grouped under several headings. These include preparation and planning, process, and outcome.

Preparation and planning

Particularly in the training phase, but also at later stages, preparation and planning are often given particular prominence and supervisors of students, or heads and senior teachers, will scrutinise some of the artefacts connected with preparation, like work schemes, lesson plans and the extent to which assessment and monitoring of pupils' work and progress have taken place not only after a lesson, but also before it. It is a widely held assumption that pre-planning is an important part of successful teaching, and sometimes teachers can be judged more on the artefacts than the lessons.

Yet there are teachers who claim to be successful at teaching intuitively and responsively, rather than on the basis of a carefully predetermined plan. This claim may simply mean, however, that they do not operate to a written plan and that their actions are determined by deep, rather than surface structures. For example, a teacher who regularly makes jokes during a lesson is not operating to a written plan, because many jokes arise spontaneously from unpredicted situations. It is more likely that deep in the teacher's subconscious belief system is a conviction that humour can reduce tension and maintain or arouse interest.

Meticulous preparation in itself does not ensure that learning will take place, but the observer can nevertheless focus on an important aspect of the quality of classroom life, namely the extent to which the teacher's original intentions or plans are actually implemented. This focus of concern can apply both in lessons that are tightly structured and presented and in those that are not. Some teachers believe that children should have a considerable say in what happens in lessons and that assignments, procedures and activities should be negotiated, not imposed. Observers can provide valuable feedback about whether or not this aspiration was translated into action. Such feedback can be offered with or without advice about the appropriateness of the pre-planning or whether keeping to or modifying the original plan was sensible.

Process

The judgements that observers with different perspectives make about classroom processes are also of interest when the indicators of quality and effectiveness are under review. Some observers enter the classroom with a clear idea of what processes they favour or dislike. Their personal reaction to a lesson might include such diverging expectations and tastes as these pairs of polar opposites:

Teacher should tell	—	*Pupils should find out*
Too much noise	—	*Not enough discussion among pupils*
Teacher clearly in charge	—	*Teacher not too authoritarian*
Good lesson pace	—	*Not enough time to reflect*

One important aspect of the observer's personal view of quality or effectiveness is his or her role, standing and relationships with the person teaching the lesson. Sometimes the relationship is clearly defined. Head teachers watching a newly arrived colleague, or supervising tutors or teachers observing a trainee, however they may handle the situation or seek to disguise it, are inescapably locked into a superior–subordinate relationship. Therefore judgements about quality are sometimes expected or, if not offered directly, inferred. The remark 'I saw some pupils who were not listening to the story' would have a different impact if offered by (a) a tutor to a student on final teaching practice, or (b) a student to an experienced teacher whose lesson she has observed as part of her assignment. The actual or perceived power relationship between observer and observed is not just a sociological concept, but rather a reality that needs to be recognised.

Qualitative subjective judgement can be sharply or loosely focused. During the Teacher Education Project (Wragg 1984) in which hundreds of lessons in secondary schools were analysed, we began our class management studies by asking teachers who supervised students what they understood by 'effective' class management. Several phrases emerged on numerous occasions, including 'having a firm grip', 'keeping pupils busy' and 'being in charge'. There was often an assumption that everyone shared the same understanding of these phrases, yet when we moved from interviews to asking people to collect and record 'critical events', a procedure described later in this chapter which involves looking for classroom events that illustrate whatever the observer is studying, there was often disagreement between supervisors.

One example illustrates this well. A student teacher, supervised by two different people, was regarded by the first of these as insensitive in his manner towards pupils. This emerged from interview and from the critical events recorded. However, the second supervisor recorded one critical event which appeared on the surface to be identical to those reported by the first supervisor. The class was studying a piece of writing from a novel and one pupil was very critical of it. The teacher asked to know why. The boy replied that it was not written in the sort of language that people would employ nowadays. When pressed to explain what expression might replace it in contemporary language, the boy replied, 'That

Figure 3.2 Two different interpretations – firm management or put-down?

funky music from down the road'. The teacher went on to say, 'That's typical of the answer I'd expect from someone who gets as low marks as you do'.

The actual event recorded by the second supervisor was very similar to those recorded by the first supervisor, but what was different was the interpretation and evaluation of the two people. Whereas the first supervisor deplored the student teacher's manner, the second supervisor wrote about the event described above, 'What I like about him is that he stands for no nonsense from any potential trouble makers'. For him the event was illustrative of the teacher's *competence*, not lack of it. This focus on specific classroom events brought out very sharply the difference in perceptions of quality of the two supervisors reporting on similar looking episodes.

Outcome

One of the factors affecting judgement about classroom processes is the observer's assessment of the likely outcome of what is witnessed. If there is not to be any systematic measurement of the results of the process of teaching and learning, then consideration has to be given to estimates of such matters as whether or not children appear to be learning. In this context learning can include not only factual knowledge, but also skills, attitudes and behaviour. The observer makes an intelligent guess about aspects of learning that can be important, and sometimes easy to appraise, like whether what is being taught is factually accurate, but sometimes more diffuse and less easy to define exactly, like whether what is being done is:

worthwhile	of value and importance, however they may be defined
coherent	links in with other concepts/activities
influential on future behaviour	like stimulating a longer term or even lifelong interest in the topic/activity
needed by society	makes a contribution to present and future citizenship
appropriate	suitable for the particular child or group in the context of the topic/subject being studied

It is often the perceived relationship between process and outcome that forms the heart of any discussion of a lesson with the teacher concerned after it is over. This is when observers may refer to any notes they have made during the lesson. There are numerous possible ways of keeping a record of the lesson observed. Some observers note down as an *aide-mémoire* anything that catches their attention as it occurs, often about process, but also about possible outcome. Examples from observers' notes when lesson evaluation is involved frequently contain comments like the following assorted collection:

'Bright opening with many pupils taking part'
'Teacher reprimands wrong child'

'Pupils work assiduously in groups'
'Teacher consistently mispronounces the *ü* sound in the word '*über*'
'Pupils in far corner constantly distract children on next table'
'Most children appear to have mastered the concept, which was clearly explained'
'The two pupils in the corner were clearly confused about the notion of a *fair test*,
    and the teacher ought to have gone over and clarified it with them'
'Check with teacher if everyone's homework had been marked'
'Teacher should have monitored children's experiments earlier'
'We must discuss possible follow-up activities'
'Introduction went on too long'
'Excellent response to story'
'Friendly manner'
'Lesson began at 10 : 15'
'Roughly equal numbers of boys and girls in class'
'Class restless, pace too slow'
'It would have been better to have some practical work at this stage as some
    children needed concrete experience'
'Teacher allows boys to rush towards computers and girls find it difficult to get a turn'
'Uses language that is too difficult for class if not explained, like *respiration*'

These comments are of many kinds. Some are fairly neutral in tone, like the note recording the time the lesson started. Others contain a positive or negative judgement by the observer, expressed in words such as 'wrong', 'should have' or 'excellent'. Certain remarks deal with several diverse, if sometimes related elements, like class management (e.g. the control of children's behaviour, monitoring of pupils' work, timing of activities), personality characteristics (friendly manner), specific content (modern language teacher's mispronunciation, story telling, science experiment, including, in the case of the comment on *respiration*, language register), teaching strategies (practical work), the pupils' activities or perspectives (girls not getting a fair chance to use computers), actual events (reprimanding wrong pupil).

Some notes flag a possible post-lesson discussion point. In a large-scale study of over 1,000 teachers involved in appraisal (Wragg *et al.* 1996), we found that freehand notes, written down as the lesson developed, were the most common form of record made by appraisers, some 75 per cent of them saying that this is what they did. Such informal records, as opposed to those put down under predetermined headings, will often be logged in the order of occurrence, rather than in conceptual groups. Part of the art of lesson analysis is to make sense of what happens, to see and explore the lesson's shape and direction, make and draw out inferences, as well as talk about possible future action.

There is a problem with defining what constitutes quality, because of the considerable variations in individual beliefs and expectations, and all the other reservations and caveats about the appraisal of quality and effectiveness expressed above. In the face of these problems it is easy to settle for saying little. Yet many teachers when observed *expect* some kind of evaluation from the observer, not a series of reasons why nothing can be said. Student teachers, experienced practitioners who rarely have an outsider present, particularly one with professional insights or able to offer and discuss examples of practice from many classrooms, or anyone teaching new subject matter or breaking fresh ground, may be desperate to know what they can do to improve their professional skill. There will be further discussion of such topics as lesson appraisal and supervision in Chapters 4 and 6, but for the moment qualitative observers might bear the following points in mind:

1   **The *purpose* of the observation should be made clear**
    Observers must make clear to the teacher being observed whether they are there to offer advice and help improve professional skill, merely to make a private judgement about quality, or, in the case of certain research projects, for example, not to make any kind of personal value judgement about quality, but simply record what is happening for future analysis. Unless the purpose of the observation is clarified a certain amount of confusion is bound to occur.

2   **The need to reflect on the nature of quality and effectiveness**
    Observers need to think about their own views on what is effective teaching (see Activity 6) and recognise that there are often several opinions about quality, not just one's own.

3   **The different ways of discussing and enhancing quality**
    After the lesson observation there is often a conversation about quality between the teacher and the observer. Thought needs to be given about how this might be structured, whether the teacher or the observer should lead, what aspects should be discussed and who decides the agenda, a matter discussed in more detail in Chapters 4 and 6.

4   **The nature of the lesson record**
    What, if anything, the observer should write down at the time or later; whether this should be under preconceived headings, like 'class management' or 'relationships', or simply noted freehand as events occur. The extent to which the record should focus on the teacher, the pupils, both; on personal traits, events, strategies, process or outcome; how evaluative the comments should be.

ACTIVITY 6

Prepare for a lesson observation in a particular field which is of interest to you, perhaps an early years infants class, a lesson on writing an imaginative story with 9 year olds, a gymnastics lesson with 11 year olds, a secondary school foreign language class, the teaching of a vocational subject in a workshop or an A level chemistry practical session in a laboratory. Decide what sort of qualitative record of the lesson you will keep. Discuss with others, if possible, what criteria of effectiveness you might look for.

Try to carry out one or more lesson observations using the approach you have chosen and discuss the lesson afterwards with the teacher concerned. How closely did you keep to your intentions? If you varied these, why did you do so? (There is no reason why you should not have done, it is just worth considering what led you to change your original intentions.) What sort of points did you note in your written record – classroom events? What people said? Pupil behaviour? Teaching strategies? What words in your account reveal your own evaluation? (Look for evaluative words like 'good', 'poor', 'correct', 'wrong', 'appropriate', 'unsuitable', as well as other words and phrases that reveal your own preferences, again without feeling that they are necessarily incorrect assumptions, simply to check what are the colourings and hues of your interpretations.)

What did you talk to the teacher about afterwards? Who initiated and who reacted? To what extent did the teacher's evaluation concur or disagree with your own appraisal? What was the mood of the post-lesson discussion – deferential? Dismissive? Apprehensive? Animated? Positive? What have you learned about appraising teacher quality and effectiveness from this exercise?

Critical events

One approach which allows the observer to capture and preserve some of the essence of what is happening in lessons is the 'critical events' technique that I have often used in classroom observation for both teacher appraisal and research (Wragg 1984, 1993a; Wragg *et al.* 1996, 1998). The observer looks for specific instances of classroom behaviour which are judged to be illustrative of some salient aspect of the teacher's style or strategies: an element of class management, for example, perhaps a rule being established, followed, or being broken, something that reflects interpersonal relationships or some other indicative event. The 'critical events' approach is based on the 'critical incidents' technique developed by Flanagan (1949). The observer writes down on a pro forma what led up to the event, what happened and what the outcome was.

After the lesson, teachers can be interviewed and asked for their perception of what happened. The interviewer uses neutral language like 'Can you tell me about …?', rather than loaded or leading questions, such as 'Why didn't you …?'. Depending on the circumstances the observer may also be able to talk to some children, but it is important that observers act in an ethical manner and ensure that the head and teachers concerned are fully in agreement with children being interviewed. Talking to children either directly or indirectly about their teachers is not something that should be undertaken without permission, and even if agreement is secured, any interviews should be conducted in a sensitive manner.

Critical event number _____   Name of teacher _____

Class _____   Date _____

What led up to the event?

What happened?

What was the outcome?

Interview with participants

The following critical event taken from a science lesson given by a student teacher in a secondary school showed up an important aspect of student teachers' class management problems. The student began the science practical lesson in a relaxed manner, describing the sort of experiment the class was going to do. The critical event, noted after about ten minutes had elapsed, happened when he instructed the pupils to begin the experiment working in pairs. 'You know what to do, so get out the gear and start your experiment,' he said, whereupon several of the boys raced towards the cupboards, seized pieces of equipment, some wrestling with each other over who should have which bunsen burner. The student had to shout to obtain order and reprimand some of the people playing tug o' war with a bunsen burner rubber tube.

The observer noted this down as an example of the teacher's response to what later became a series of disorderly events in an unruly lesson. After the lesson he asked the question 'Can you tell me a bit about what happened when you asked the children to get out the equipment?' (rather than 'when the children started fooling around'). The student teacher then explained how he was simply imitating the casual way in which he had seen the class's regular science teacher start experiments. However, it became clear that he had visited the school to watch some lessons in December, after the school had been in session for three months. By then the class's regular teacher had forged a well-established friendly

'Now let's see if we can find some positive points, Mr Sanderson'

Figure 3.3 Teacher appraisal

Figure 3.4 Critical event – disorder in the lab

relationship and was able to be relaxed and jocular. The student assumed that he could imitate this manner, but was unaware of the considerable efforts made by the class's teacher in the previous September to ensure that pupils did not misbehave, establish ground rules and enforce these in a consistent manner. It was only after he had impressed on pupils how they must behave in a laboratory, that he had adopted a much more informal manner. This critical event, and the interviews with the student and class teacher, highlighted the problem faced by student teachers inheriting styles and procedures whose origins they have not been able to witness.

Critical events need not be spectacular. They are simply things that happen that seem to the observer to be of more interest than other events occurring at the same time, and therefore worth documenting in greater detail, usually because they tell a small but significant part of a larger story. It is not easy to collect, discuss and analyse more than about three such events in an observation session, but intelligent selection can enhance post-lesson discussion or analysis of someone's teaching.

Body language

Learning to use one's eyes with sharp discrimination is an important part of the craft of lesson observation. Although a great deal of attention is rightly given to what is *said* in the classroom, there are many other messages put out by people to one another during communication that are worthy of note. Non-verbal aspects of classroom behaviour include posture, movement, gesture, facial expression and eye contact. In making decisions about what to do, both teachers and pupils will rapidly scan faces and body postures, search their memory for information about previous encounters with the same individuals or similar circumstances, and then decide how to act, all within less than a second on some occasions. It is an astonishing example of human beings' capacity to process information at speed.

The term 'body language' is but one expression used to cover non-verbal behaviour. It sometimes focuses exclusively on aspects such as posture, which can be quite important in classrooms, but there are other elements which must be considered. Posture can reveal interest, threat, boredom, excitement, a whole range of human emotions. Teachers of small children usually crouch alongside them to minimise the height difference, but when they are angry they may draw themselves up to their full height, maximising the height difference to establish or maintain dominance.

Posture can signal impending movement, so that people will flinch, for example, if they see someone's posture change, a shift of weight maybe, that suggests attack. Teachers sometimes use movement to counter or even offer threat, so they may move rapidly towards someone who is misbehaving. This quick shortening of social distance, and invasion of someone else's personal space, often conveys the suggestion of possible attack, even though children know, rationally, that teachers are not allowed to strike them.

Gestures are also used to amplify meaning, but teachers use them for different purposes. A moving pointed finger may illustrate the line of a graph or the timing of a musical rhythm. Both hands may be used to indicate the width of an object, to pacify someone who is angry or over-excited ('Calm it down') or to illustrate the movement of a seesaw. In addition to these more low key uses the hands may also signal aggression through the jabbing or accusing finger, suggestive of a club that could physically assault. Look at the pictures of hand movements in Figure 3.6 and see what they suggest to the person in receipt of the communication – anger? Encouragement? Enlightenment? Intimidation? Bewilderment?

Figure 3.5 Crouching alongside and towering over children

Figure 3.6 What do hands reveal?

Figure 3.7 Eye contact

Facial expressions convey added meaning, as numerous small muscles twist the face into different casts, illustrating embarrassment, happiness, apprehension or scorn. Some of these facial responses, like the reddening blush, are innate rather than learned, as blind people can blush even though they have never seen a red face to imitate. Other facial expressions are learned socially. Eyes are one of the most important elements of non-verbal and verbal communication, and teachers will not only scan across the room to see what is happening, or focus on an individual pupil, but also engage children in eye contact in an attempt to read from their eyes what they are thinking. Sometimes lack of eye contact can lead to the teacher not picking up that some pupils have lost interest, or that they have finished their work and are trying to catch the teacher's attention.

Lesson observers often do not write down the detail of non-verbal behaviour, but it does inform their judgement. Some people would not record 'Teacher stands with hands clasped tightly under armpits close to blackboard looking insecure', but would reach a conclusion on the evidence of such visual body cues without necessarily articulating it. The same applies to movement. Many observers do not record detail about teachers' or pupils' movements, but some do, especially where they reveal important aspects of classroom life, like that the teacher moved round the room monitoring different children's work, or that pupils were permitted freedom of movement provided they behaved well.

One caveat about the interpretation of body language is that it can be mistaken. Some postures, facial expressions, movements can be ambiguous – the smile that could reveal nervousness or confidence, the pupil who appears to be either day-dreaming or planning the next move, the frown of confusion or the grimace of anger. We often perceive exactly what transmitters of messages and signals want us to perceive, otherwise, were there too much ambiguity, millions of motorists and pedestrians would be killed every day. However, there are major and minor accidents and disasters in life, and sometimes these are the direct result of ambiguities, or of misinterpretations of moods and messages. Look at Figure 3.8 and see if you feel certain or uncertain about what is portrayed.

Analysing transcripts and lesson accounts

The end product of many qualitative observations is a notebook full of written field notes, a set of sound or video cassettes, a collection of well-documented critical events, or simply an *aide-mémoire* of points the observer wants to discuss with the teacher. The shelves of many an appraiser's or researcher's study groan under the weight of unanalysed notebooks or tapes. In many ways the notes and tapes that remain undiscussed or unheard for more than a week may never again see the light of day, for the more time that elapses, the less likely it is that anyone will either understand the significance of them, or be motivated to revisit them, once direct and immediate memory have faded. *Analyse qualitative records as soon as possible* is the message.

Language in the classroom is a very important issue which has been addressed in major reports and by several writers in the field, including Sinclair and Coulthard (1975), Stubbs (1983) and Edwards and Westgate (1987). Transcripts of classroom discourse can be analysed either qualitatively or quantitatively, and earlier sections of this book have mentioned some possibilities. However, despite the evolution of computer packages for performing content analysis on transcripts, many people prefer the painstaking personal scrutiny of what people have said, which is why so many transcripts remain unanalysed.

Once transcripts are available there are several aspects of language that can be considered. Some observers are interested in the difference between classroom language and the language of the playground or the home. Tizard and Hughes (1984) analysed not only the conversations between teachers and young children, but also those between the same children and their own parents. They found that there was a more elaborate language exchange in the home than in the nursery school, and that if one looked at what happened during story time, either in the home or the school, children asked numerous questions of their parent, but very few of their teacher. Other observers might be interested in dialect, curious to know what happens when pupils use non-standard forms, like 'I haven't done nothing', where the double negative is incorrect in standard English, but may be acceptable as a means of emphasis in the playground or the home, as indeed happens in a language like French (*ne ... rien, ne ... jamais*).

Teachers and pupils may talk at 100 to 150 words a minute, occasionally faster, depending on how rapid the interaction is. Even in 30 minutes there can be 10 to

Figure 3.8 Ambiguous body language

Figure 3.9 Language in the classroom and the home

20 pages of transcript. Anyone seeking to draw inferences from the transcripts of several lesson observations could be faced with hundreds of pages of text. It is not for the fainthearted, and observers need to be clear in their minds why they might want such detail. There are numerous possible reasons and there are different approaches for different purposes, such as the following, most of which apply to the analysis of transcripts, field notes as well as critical events. Clarifying purposes and then choosing appropriate strategies is an essential first step.

Purpose   Identifying salient points in the lesson, for comment or discussion.
Strategy   Read text and use highlighter pen to identify statements worthy of note, and then group these under suitable headings. This can be done either when discussing a teacher's lesson with the person concerned, or when conducting research to elicit pupils' and teachers' understandings and interpretations of what happens in classrooms.

Purpose   Seeing whether pupils had an opportunity to learn a particular matter.
Strategy   Scan text to find instances where the particular topic or concept was discussed. For example, if a child does not know that magnets pick up objects with iron in them, look back at the section of the lesson when magnetism was discussed to see if this was mentioned. It may then turn out that the issue never came up at all, that it was described in ambiguous or unclear form, or that it was indeed mentioned, but the child concerned perhaps did not hear, was not paying attention, or could not understand.

Purpose   Looking at the teacher's language register to see how appropriate it is for the topic and pupils concerned.
Strategy   Search the text for examples of teacher explaining to child or group, to see whether the choice of words and expressions was appropriate to the individual or group concerned.

Purpose   Studying individual classroom episodes to see what impact these might have had on the pupils.
Strategy   Identify what appear to be the beginning and end of an episode, and then follow through the sequence of talk to see what happened and how it might be explained, possibly with follow-up interview with the teacher and/or pupils concerned. This is useful when trying to obtain teachers' or pupils' comments on events, as the actual words can be discussed. However, it needs to be done as soon after the lesson as possible, otherwise memories become distorted, and this is one of the problems that occur if lesson transcripts take a long time to be assembled and collected.

Similar possibilities exist when observers carrying out research have collected together critical events or freehand notes and want to elicit a pattern, extract principles, or select illustrative examples for their account of what happened in the lessons they saw. Empirical enquiry of this kind, where the researcher starts with the data, what is seen and recorded, and then elicits the theory or the questions or the propositions, is time consuming and can be extremely subjective. Grounding one's inferences in what was actually observed, as opposed to the approach of the rationalists and classical humanists who begin with theories and propositions and then see if the data fit them, is a tradition that goes back at least as far as Comenius, the seventeenth-century education reformer, who advocated studying the heaven, the earth, oaks and beeches before books. The use of these kinds of qualitative methods in research projects will be considered once more in Chapter 5.

Quantifying the qualitative

Many observers working entirely in the qualitative tradition of observation and analysis would not, under any circumstances, wish to quantify what they had seen. Indeed the very thought would be anathema to them. However, some observers do find that they want to put their field notes into some kind of systematic shape which may involve a certain amount of quantification, and there are procedures which will accommodate this. One procedure is to have the observer's notes, often known as a lesson *protocol*, typed out in line format with each single line separately numbered, and then analyse these one by one. It is a technique pioneered by, among others, Berliner and Tikunoff (1976) in the California Beginning Teacher Evaluation Study. There are several possibilities, just one of which is shown below, based on the following lesson protocol from an observation during a research project (Wragg 1993a).

Protocol	I	*School*	Midtown First School
Researcher	ECW	*Teacher*	Mrs K (and supply Mrs M)
Date	Day I of school year	*Observation*	8:30 a.m. onwards
Setting	First Encounters Study		
	City of Somewhere, Midtown Estate		
	Midtown First School Room 2		
	Reception class, first day arrival of new pupils		
	23 children (12 boys, 11 girls)		
	Six tables for children, two tables for equipment, teacher's desk		

1 The school is a large nursery and first school for 3 to 8 year olds in the
2 middle of a huge working-class estate. From 8:30 onwards children arrive,
3 some alone, some in twos and threes, sometimes with, sometimes without
4 their parents. Whole families appear, mother, grandma, grandad, the child
5 starting school, often a younger brother or sister, maybe two, with one in a
6 push chair, even the family dog. It is a big family occasion. By nine a.m.
7 most children are in school and the street outside is deserted apart from the
8 occasional passer-by or late arrival. Mrs A has about two-thirds of her class
9 present. She sits in a chair with the children around her feet. They talk about
10 dinners, classroom rituals, who knows who in the class and where children

11   might sit. Every five minutes or so a parent appears at the door with a child.
12   An extra teacher, brought in for the first week, is on hand to feed in the
13   latecomers. By 9:30 the class appears to be complete and children are
14   assigned to tables where they choose an activity from several possibilities ...
15   at 10:20 there is an ear-splitting yell from down the corridor. The last arrival
16   has appeared. She is clearly not enamoured of the idea of coming to school
17   and her cries of 'No, mummy, I don't want to go' are joined in counterpoint
18   by her mother's audible threats, bribes and oaths, 'I'll come and fetch you at
19   tea time', 'You've *got* to go to school or I'll get into trouble.' Outside Mrs
20   A's classroom the extra supply teacher attempts to soothe parent and child.
21   What's her name? Tina is it? Well, come with me Tina and I'll take you
22   into Mrs A's room.' Tina kicks her violently on the shin.
23   The supply teacher brings Tina and her mother into the classroom. She sits
24   Tina down at a table and starts to do a jigsaw with her. 'I'm just going to
25   have a word with Mrs A, I'll be back in a second.' Meanwhile, Tina's
26   mother slips gratefully out of the room. A brief ten second conversation
27   between the supply teacher and Mrs A follows, in which the supply teacher
28   says she will leave Tina to get on with the jigsaw. She returns to the table and
29   crouches alongside Tina, 'Oh well done, you're good at jigsaws, aren't you,
30   Tina?' With that she mutters a vague, 'I'll be back soon' and leaves the
31   room. A couple of minutes later Mrs A goes over to Tina. 'You've nearly
32   finished that Tina, well done. Here's a box of building bricks. When you've
33   finished see if you can build something nice and then I'll come and have a
34   look at it ...'
35   For the whole of the day Tina worked assiduously alongside the rest of the
36   class, slightly reserved, but indistinguishable from the others, doing the
37   activities, eating her lunch, playing in the playground during breaks.
38   The supply teacher made a brief return visit to see how she was, but by then
39   she was immersed in constructing an elaborate arrangement of building bricks
40   and barely looked up. At 3:15 she listened attentively as the teacher read the
41   class a story, congratulated the children on their good behaviour and said she
42   was looking forward to seeing them all the following day. At 3:30 the bell
43   rang for the end of school and parents clustered outside the classroom to
44   collect their children. Tina's mother appeared, pale faced and anxiously
45   asking how she had got on. 'Fine,' replied Mrs A, 'see you tomorrow Tina',
46   whereupon Tina burst into tears. Her mother may well have been convinced
47   that she had spent the day on the rack. The following day, however, Tina
48   came to school on time, was calm in appearance and manifested no outward
49   signs of distress about school.

A pair of raters can then read the protocol independently, attempting to bring out
important aspects of it, depending on what the observer or teacher want to consider.
It could be 'dimensions of teacher effectiveness', 'pupil behaviour' or 'personal
relationships'. The dividing of the protocol into lines allows the readers to compare

their interpretations. Suppose, for example, they had both separately identified 'violence towards teacher' as an event to note, then they could check that they were both referring to line 22, 'Tina kicks her violently on the shin'. It also allows each separate line to be coded in some way.

The two readers, in looking for examples of effectiveness, might both highlight lines 23-24 and 28-30, which describe how the teacher sits with Tina and helps her become interested in a jigsaw puzzle. This might lead to categories such as 'involving pupil in task' being noted. Each line can be scrutinised to see if it occurs. A seven point scale could then be used to see whether such features as had been identified appeared to be significant in a lesson or not, using 'less' and 'more' as the dimensions of significance:

Involving pupils		1	2	3	4	5	6	7	
Warmth	less	1	2	3	4	5	6	7	more
Reprimanding		1	2	3	4	5	6	7	

Study of several such protocols might then find that in lessons thought to be effective there was more likelihood that pupils who had become distracted would be reinvolved in their work, or that there would be more personal warmth from the teacher, or a greater tendency to reprimand. The advantage of quantifying in this way is that it can sometimes lend shape to a large amount of descriptive text about what happened in lessons, and also give a certain degree of objectivity by asking readers to make judgements from the same protocol, but independently of each other. The major disadvantage is that it can reduce valuable evidence from a sophisticated and detailed account written by an intelligent observer capable of detecting fine nuances, to a set of crude categories and ciphers. Many observers in any case prefer to use a mixture of methods, and in Chapter 4 we shall consider the different purposes, settings and applications of classroom observation and the variety of ways that are employed to carry it out.

Chapter 4

Classroom observation in context

There is a strong argument that teaching should be much more open than it has previously been, with teachers themselves playing a prominent role in observing, analysing and disseminating best practice, however that might be conceived. Greater public accountability during the last three decades of the twentieth century brought schools under close scrutiny and, in some cases, critical review. It is a great pity that the tradition in a field like surgery, whereby surgeons learn from each other by studying videotapes, or watching live and even joining in as assistants, when new techniques are being developed and perfected, is not imitated more frequently in teaching. Although the surgery/teaching analogy does not always stand up to close inspection, the open sharing of new ideas and the convention of 'sitting in' with fellow practitioners are matters that could spread to teaching with profit, provided appropriate time and resources are made available.

This chapter will describe seven major contexts in which classroom observation can play a significant part in studying and determining action. These are

1   initial teacher training
2   in-service training and professional development
3   studying pupils
4   curriculum development and evaluation
5   job analysis
6   teacher appraisal
7   observation by lay people

The eighth context, the use of classroom observation for the purposes of research, will be covered in Chapter 5. All the seven fields mentioned above can, of course, themselves be the subject of research. However, much greater rigour and depth of analysis are required when carrying out research, which usually involves investigation in a systematic way, using one or more of the traditions of enquiry described in previous chapters. The emphasis in this chapter is on informal and semi-formal classroom observation for the purpose of looking at, or attempting to improve the quality of teaching and learning. Research, particularly action research and research and development (R & D) projects, can also have the same aspirations, trying to improve teaching and learning through careful enquiry, and these matters will also be addressed in Chapter 5. In Chapter 6 there will also be a number of examples of classroom observation in action in several of these fields, but for the present the emphasis is on outlining some of the possibilities for undertaking classroom observation in informal and semi-formal settings within normal resources.

Initial teacher training

Firmly fixed patterns of classroom interaction can be laid down quite early in a teacher's career, even during training; in a study of over 100 postgraduate student teachers which I conducted (Wragg 1973), it emerged that some had already established fairly stable styles of teaching even when on teaching practice. Looking at one's own or someone else's teaching, therefore, can be an important part of initial training. For many teachers, the period of their initial training was virtually the only time in their career when they were observed. Good or bad habits, first of observation, second of reflection on one's own or another student's or teacher's practice, can be fashioned during initial training.

Observing others

The tradition of observing other teachers was already well known in the nineteenth century, and in the 1830s the Scottish pioneer David Stow introduced the 'gallery lesson' into the Glasgow Normal Seminary where he taught. Trainees and their tutors watched a student teach from their seat in the gallery, hence the term 'gallery lesson'. Some literally 'played to the gallery' and showed off in front of their fellows.

Nowadays there are two regular opportunities for trainees to watch teaching, the first is live observation of lessons in schools, the second is studying video-tapes of classrooms. It is a useful exercise for trainees to watch a good video of one or more teachers at work in their own classroom. The opportunity to stop and start the tape, speculate about consequences, or discuss outcomes away from the pressure of taking a class, can raise important matters of principle and practice. The development of various forms of interactive technology is an extension of this facility, offering a high quality of picture, as well as the ability to hold or 'freeze' a single frame and study a still life picture of the classroom. Most of all, because interactive technology can handle both print and pictures, provide speedy responses and be subject to monitoring by a tutor, there are rich possibilities for individual and small group self-supported tutorial work.

One interactive option that is liked by student teachers is the 'interrupted story', when a classroom scene is played and the individual or group can then select one of a number of options and see the consequences of their choice. For example, the scene may show a pupil misbehaving. When the film stops the trainee is invited to make a choice: (a) to ignore it, (b) to punish the child, (c) to reinvolve the child in the work, or (d) to discuss the misbehaviour with the pupil concerned and others. Having made a selection the trainee can then see filmed consequences of the choice. The major problem with this neat looking approach is that the film maker or director may have simply programmed personal prejudices into the story line. If someone believes that it is 'best' to reinvolve pupils in their work, then when they film the consequence of this choice of action it is easy for them to portray a positive outcome. Inexperienced trainees might then assume all similar problems have the same solution. Nonetheless, the immense storage capacity available through interactive technology, with high quality pictures, rapid access and immediate response, offer a variety of possibilities to discuss dilemmas and decisions, if sensibly handled. When it is functioning properly, interactive technology has several positive qualities, but technical problems can be a source of frustration to tutor and students.

With trainees early in their training programme, when they observe a teacher live in the classroom, it might be best either to use a simple set of headings, or to invite them to make freehand notes. A simple structure for looking at the strategies of questioning and explaining, either in their own teaching, or when watching an experienced teacher, might look like the one below. Several student teachers can use the same structure and then compare their observations, either of the same lesson, or of different ones. They can also interview the teacher concerned, or talk to the pupils, to see whether they have understood events, if the teacher agrees.

QUESTION LOG

A *Questions asked*   Write down three questions asked during the observation period and the responses obtained. In each case write the actual words of the question and the sort of response obtained.

Question 1 _____

Response _____

_____

Question 2 _____

Response _____

_____

Question 3 _____

Response _____

_____

B *Sequences*   Write down a sequence of between two and five questions that belonged together and followed each other. Write the actual words asked and brief notes about the reasons behind the sequence and the actual outcome.

Question 1 _____

Outcome _____

_____

_____

Question 2 _____

Outcome _____

Question 3 _____

Question 4 _____

Question 5 _____

Your reflections on the sequence

EXPLANING LOG

C *Explanations* Write down two explanations given, either to the whole class, a small group, or an individual pupil. Describe the context, the strategy used and what the result was.

Explanation 1

Explanation 2

D *Explaining to different pupils* Write down an explanation given to a more able and a less able pupil during the day. In each case note the context, the strategy used and the outcome.

Explanation to more able pupil

Explanation to less able pupil

It is important to have an agenda for discussing these logs with fellow students or teachers/tutors, otherwise a shapeless discussion without focus can take place. There are several ways of reflecting on what different observers have discovered about their teaching. These include the following possibilities:

1 Teachers take it in turn to talk about the purposes and content of some of their questions/explanations.
2 Members of the group try to see what points of substance they can learn from each other's strategies.
3 Look at any common features (e.g. use of vocabulary and language register when explaining to more and less able pupils, to see what seemed effective and ineffective).
4 Persuade some members of the group to video lessons when they are asking questions or explaining a new topic and discuss ways of improving what is done.
5 Ask an individual to explain a personal interest to the rest of the group (a favourite painting/piece of music, how to play backgammon, the joys of fell walking, running your own finances, a scientific principle, how a car engine works, making your own pasta). Then discuss how you would explain

Figure 4.1 Should you call on only those who raise their hands?

the same topic: (a) to a 6 year old, (b) to a 13 year old, (c) to an intelligent Martian.

6   Discuss personal views with other people on matters such as: (a) should you call only on children who put up their hand to answer, or sometimes address others, (b) what options are open to you when you don't know the answer (e.g. a child asks why some grains of sand float, even though most sink to the bottom of the water container), (c) how you might react when children answer incorrectly (Give them another chance? Ask someone else? Give them a clue?).

The research evidence on the effectiveness of different micro-strategies in questioning and explaining is by no means conclusive, so there is a great deal of scope for discussion and exploration of various possible alternatives.

Pair working

One effective way for both novices and experienced teachers to collaborate is for them to work as a pair with a specific agenda. Each acts as teacher and observer, using the identical approach. Activity 7 shows how two trainees or a trainee and a supervising teacher or tutor can engage in such reciprocal pair work to improve their vigilance in class. The observer learns to look carefully to find children not engaged in the task, the person teaching, knowing what the observer is doing, becomes very vigilant.

ACTIVITY 7

A *Eyes* For ten minutes watch the teacher's use of eyes, looking in particular for: (1) *eye contact* or lack of it, and (2) use of eyes to *sweep across the class*. Make notes about how the teacher uses his/her eyes.

B *Pupils not engaged in the task* Look for two pupils who appear not to be engaged in the task, for whatever reason. Study each one for five minutes and make notes below about what each child does.

Pupil 1

Pupil 2

C *Discussion* Discuss what has been observed with the teacher and then swap roles, so that observer becomes teacher and vice versa.

Supervision and mentoring

As partnerships between schools and training institutions have developed, the process of supervision of trainees has come under much more scrutiny. One common feature of initial training is the discussion of what has been observed with the person regarded as the student's 'mentor'. This term has often been used to describe a teacher responsible for the professional development of a student in the school, but the word 'mentor' is a generic term referring to anyone who influences the development of someone else's mind, so it can equally be used for a tutor from a training institution. Student teachers react differently to their mentor, some with affection and respect, others with contempt or even apprehension. The mentor-student relationship is crucial, and negative stories often result either from a supervisor feeling that the student is rigid, arrogant, lazy or unwilling to take advice, or from the student complaining that post-lesson critiques concentrate on negative aspects and do not bring out the positive. Very capable students sometimes feel let down if the mentor simply says, 'That's fine' or 'You're very good', as they too want to improve.

McIntyre (1977) looked at supervision in three different contexts: students taught lessons which were videotaped, and they were then invited to analyse their lesson either with a tutor, or with other students in groups of three. Students tended to prefer a tutor to be present. If students do want dialogue with a supervisor, then supervision is in itself a craft which observers who are also responsible for students' professional development need to develop, and exploring various styles of post-lesson analysis is just as important for supervisors, as trying out different styles of teaching is for teachers. Stones (1984) argues that supervision is a greatly neglected craft and one that should lie at the centre of developing teaching skills and understanding how children learn. Some possibilities include the following:

1   The mentor gives an analytical account of the lesson and asks the student to comment.
2   The student gives an analytical account of the lesson and the mentor comments.
3   The mentor and student hold an unstructured or semi-structured conversation about the lesson, with neither taking a dominant role.
4   The mentor collects critical events and then discusses these with the student.
5   The mentor makes a sound tape or video of a lesson and then plays it back with the student, stopping and starting it whenever one of the two participants wishes to talk about what is happening.
6   The mentor uses some agreed checklist or set of headings to complete a pro forma which is then discussed.
7   The mentor chooses positive and negative aspects of the lesson, as he/she sees it, and then feeds back either the positive ones first, to avoid undermining the student's confidence, or the negative ones first, to get them out of the way.

There are as many styles of supervision as there are supervisors, and most use a variety of approaches. Mentors need to be aware of two tendencies. The first is to *project themselves as a paragon ideal*, that is to imagine themselves teaching flawlessly the class they are observing, forgetting their own errors and infelicities. This can give rise to a temptation to take over to show how it should be done, or to talk entirely in terms of their own preferred strategies. The second is the tendency to *compensate for their own deficiencies*, that is to feel they must correct particularly strongly any aspect in which they are themselves weak, for example, tidiness, or the use of visual aids. Mutual trust and respect are essential ingredients for a healthy relationship between supervisor and student.

Micro-teaching

One of the biggest problems facing those who train new teachers is the sheer complexity of teaching in a busy classroom. The purpose of micro-teaching in its many forms is to reduce this complexity so that the newcomer has the opportunity to concentrate on one particular aspect or skill at a time. The basic format for micro-teaching was originally developed at Stanford University in the 1960s (Allen and Ryan 1969). It was an attempt to scale down classroom life so that trainees could develop one aspect of their skill with a small number of children, rather than have to work at everything with thirty pupils to teach. Although there have been numerous versions of micro-teaching since its early development, there are usually eight features:

1   *Preparation* The student prepares a short lesson, usually around ten minutes in length, often in the light of preliminary discussion with supervisor, attempting to concentrate on some aspect of teaching and learning.

2   *Skills*   Particular attention is devoted to one aspect of teaching proficiency, like class management, explaining, or questioning.

3   *Class size*   A small group of children, from three up to half a class is taught.

4   *Time unit*   A small amount of time is common, often from five up to twenty minutes, for the student to teach the class and be videotaped.

5   *'Teach' phase*   The student has a first attempt at teaching the group.

6   *Feedback*   The student receives feedback (from a supervising teacher or tutor, fellow students, children's written responses to a questionnaire about what they have experienced, or from watching the videotape).

7   *'Reteach' phase*   The student has a second opportunity, often with a parallel group of children from the same class, to teach the same topic, but this time in the light of feedback and reflection.

8   *Debriefing*   After the full cycle has been completed the student has an opportunity to discuss what has been learned and reflect on future teaching strategies.

An illustration from a micro-teaching session right at the beginning of a trainee teacher's course, illustrates the potential when the process goes well:

Helen has, with enormous care, prepared a lesson on volcanoes. She teaches the first lesson by giving the class a number of pieces of information about the nature of volcanoes: Today I want to tell you a little bit about volcanoes. Here is a model of one and you can see that this is the crater and, as you probably know, this is the lava, and this part here is called the magma chamber. Perhaps you've heard of volcanoes before. There's one in Italy called Vesuvius. ...'

When she watches the videotape she is disappointed by the class's poor response on the rare opportunities she has given them to contribute. Her supervisor suggests she might start the reteach phase with the second group of children by simply asking the class what they know about volcanoes and following up from this. Gradually, after a few hesitant responses, more children contribute, referring to television programmes, their friends' and parents' holiday and travel experiences, things they have read in books, mentioning Vesuvius, Etna, the dust from Krakatoa travelling several times around the Earth, craters on the moon, Icelandic geysers and various other notions, using terms like 'lava' and 'eruption'. Helen is delighted, but also surprised by the breadth and depth of their existing knowledge.

It is not always the case that the second lesson is 'better'; indeed it is arguable whether Helen's first lesson was necessarily 'worse' than her reteach. What is important, however, is the opportunity to learn about teaching and explore alternatives in an environment where there is time to do it properly. There are several reservations about micro-teaching, however, which need to be considered. First of all it is very labour-intensive and demanding on supervising teachers or tutors, which is why it has not been as widespread as was originally hoped by its instigators. It has also been criticised for being artificial, too unlike 'real' classrooms, for atomising teaching into separate discrete skills, when, according to its critics, teaching should be seen as an organic whole, and for emphasising the performance elements of teaching, the presentation skills, rather than such matters as listening to pupils, or sitting and talking to an individual.

Figure 4.2 Micro-teaching – 'Teach' and 'Reteach' phases

There is another important point about the videotaping of trainees and that is about what might be called 'self-confrontation', inspecting oneself in some way. There is an assumption that if teachers could only see themselves, they would *ipso facto* improve. Nothing could be further from the truth. Although some people are perfectly able to look at themselves on video and pick out aspects they can make more effective, others become tense and find their self-confidence is undermined. We carry around with us a self-image which can be rudely shattered when we see ourselves on video for the first time and realise we are just as frail as the rest of humanity. It is essential, therefore, that students should see themselves on video more than once, in order to overcome what is sometimes known as the 'cosmetic effect' ('Don't I look awful'). Anyone analysing videos, either with beginners or for that matter with experienced teachers, should proceed thoughtfully and sensitively. The act of teaching is inseparable from the whole person and to attack the one is to demolish the other.

It is well worth while trainees having their own individual videotape from the beginning of their course, and they will then be able to assemble, during their training, a collection of scenes from their own classroom experiences, giving them a unique record of their personal and professional development. Like other forms of lesson observation and analysis in initial training, micro-teaching and the videotaping of lessons is something that, if skilfully handled, can be a valuable element in student teachers' early learning processes, but done in a ham-fisted manner can be counter-productive.

In-service training and professional development

Many of the points made about initial training apply to the further professional development of experienced teachers. They too can work in pairs, see themselves on videotape, look at lesson protocols and transcripts, and study videotapes of other teachers' lessons. Indeed, going to someone else's classroom to observe practice is often highly esteemed by teachers on the occasions, somewhat rare, unfortunately, that they have for such visits. Those responsible for professional development programmes in school would do well to arrange visits to classrooms, when possible to other schools, not just their own, as seeing others at work can be a valuable component of staff development policy and practice.

Furthermore the link between classroom observation for initial training and for in-service purposes can be a strong one. It is difficult for teachers to observe a student's lesson in a systematic way, looking perhaps at teacher-pupil interaction, class management strategies or lack of them, or the nature of the task being set for individual pupils, without reflecting on their own practice. Looking in a student's lesson for 'questions which invite children to formulate a hypothesis', for example, makes you wonder whether you ever ask such questions yourself, and if so, what the outcome is, or if you do not do so, why not? If student teachers did not exist it would be worth inventing them as a means of fomenting critical analysis of professional practice.

Reciprocal pair work, whereby two teachers pair up to study and observe each other, is a rich form of professional development. Most teachers prefer some degree of structure for such activities, otherwise post-lesson discussion can be bland and soothing ('Seemed fine') or unfocused. Teachers can either use an existing structure, like the ones described in Chapters 2 and 3, or negotiate a bespoke task which they both agree to be worth investigating, like the following:

1   Two infant school teachers look at how they hear children read, monitoring progress so that they can see if any changes they make lead to an improvement in children's reading ability (need to beware of simply 'teaching to the test' and manufacturing a spurious rise in reading test scores).

2   Two secondary science teachers sit in on each other's laboratory sessions to watch small groups during experimental work, noting how harmoniously or otherwise they work together, and how effectively they learn the topic (the observer can interview some of the children after the lesson to see how well they understand what they have been doing).

3   Three teachers of 5, 6 and 7 year olds watch each other's lessons (A watches B and C, B observes A and C, C watches A and B) in a similar subject or topic area (for example, technology, mathematics, science, writing, humanities projects, the use of radio and television broadcasts) to see how much continuity and coherence there appears to be in the curriculum for 5 to 7 year olds.

4   Two physical education teachers study each other's lessons, concentrating on six target pupils, two each of high, medium and low ability in PE, to document what kind of movement each does during a lesson or competitive game (video can be valuable here, if available).

Studying pupils

There is a tendency, in many of the published classroom observation schemes and handbooks, to concentrate on what the teacher does, especially when the emphasis is on the development or enhancement of teachers' classroom skills. However, it is equally enlightening to look at pupils, and some of the activities suggested in this book do precisely that. By studying what pupils do, observers can learn a great deal, not only about the impact of teaching on the learner, but also about the child's perspective and the influence that individual and groups of children have on the lesson.

Pupil pursuit

One of the most frequently used approaches to eliciting the child's eye view is to follow a single or sometimes a pair of children around for most or all of their school day, the 'pupil pursuit' as it is sometimes called. In primary schools this often involves sitting in the same room for most of the day, logging the child's activities and movements, but in secondary schools it can mean visiting seven or eight different locations. The principal intention is to capture the flavour of what it means to be a pupil in a particular class or group, without making the child concerned too self-conscious.

There are problems of selection, of course, and making generalisations about the experience of a whole class on the basis of the sole disruptive child, or the most capable pupil, would distort the true picture of events for the rest, which is why some observers choose a pair of children, or even six different target pupils, a boy and a girl from each of high, medium and low ability children. However, logging the experiences of a pupil can reveal a number of interesting aspects of classroom life.

I once took a group of student teachers to a secondary school which wanted to know more about how its language policy was working out in practice. Each student was attached to a class and target pupils were followed for the day. The students kept a detailed log of what kind of language activity was happening, noting, for example, whether each child was reading, writing, listening or talking, at various stages of the lesson. The findings were most interesting. Some children went to seven different lessons and completed seven workcards, one in each lesson. Others listened and wrote a great deal, sometimes copying from books or the blackboard, but did little practical activity, nor talked to the teacher or each other. Yet others were highly active in their use of language, reading, talking, asking questions of the teacher, discussing with fellow pupils and writing in a variety of contexts for different purposes. At the end of each of the three days of observation the students wrote a freehand account entitled 'Had I been a pupil in this class today. ...'

When the findings were fed back to the teachers in the school, a lively discussion ensued. Most had little idea of what had happened in previous lessons, so when one teacher said, in the seventh lesson of the day, 'I want you to do this workcard', the groans at death by a thousand workcards could be explained by what had happened in previous lessons. It led to the teachers reviewing their use of workcards, and also looking at the range of activities being employed with pupils in different year groups.

Sometimes, alongside a freehand diary-type record of what a pupil is doing, it is worth recording a time sample every few minutes or so of some aspect of the child's behaviour that can amplify the record. This could be a record of movement, a checking of what the child is doing at the moment of audit (reading, writing, listening, talking to a fellow pupil), or a note of what the teacher is doing and the child's part in it (or not, as the case may be). One possibility is to use the simple structure described in Chapter 2 for recording time on the task and misbehaviour. Every ten minutes or so from the beginning of the observation period, a quick check can be made, and two ticks inserted in the relevant columns.

| | Involvement level | | | | Deviancy level | | |
Time	low	medium	high		none	mild	serious
9:00	/					/	
9:10			/		/		
9:20			/		/		
9:30		/			/		
9:40			/		/		
9:50	/					/	

Groups

Another important focus on children is to study a particular group of pupils, perhaps working together on a project or activity, or sitting at the same table. There is often an assumption that children are adept at working collaboratively and will invariably profit from being alongside others. While this may be true on some occasions, there is no guarantee that group work will always be used effectively. Some children may disrupt rather than enhance what their fellows are trying to achieve. There are numerous questions which can be addressed in an exercise where small groups rather than whole classes or individuals are the main focus of attention, including the following:

1 Are the pupils working separately or collaboratively (both are perfectly permissible)?
2 How were groups assembled? Free choice? Teacher directed?
3 Are they working harmoniously, or is there discord? If so, why?
4 Does the assignment appear to be clear, or is there some confusion as to what they should be doing?
5 Is the task appropriate to the group, or is it beneath/beyond them?
6 Is the work shared evenly among members of the group, or does one child dominate and not allow others to contribute?
7 What is the role of different pupils? Are the groups single sex or mixed? Are there differences in the way that boys and girls are working?
8 How does the teacher monitor what the group is doing and what children are learning?

There are no omnipurpose 'correct' answers to these questions, as the context in which they occur is important, but they do raise issues about group work in the classroom which are worthy of discussion and further reflection and action.

Figure 4.3 Working in groups – is it a positive experience?

Curriculum development and evaluation

That teaching can be an extraordinarily busy activity, with its numerous repeated and rehearsed strategies and the frequency of its interactions, has been pointed out several times in this book. If teachers engage in a thousand or so interpersonal transactions in a single day, then it is difficult for them to step back and scrutinise what they are doing. Someone who has been teaching for five years or more will already have engaged in over a million exchanges in the classroom, and patterns of behaviour have been laid down which are not always easy to change. Yet a new curriculum or examination syllabus may require not just new subject matter to be introduced, but different strategies to be employed.

Consider some of the many changes that have been introduced into the primary and secondary curriculum in recent years, like the encouragement of investigation in mathematics, learning to construct a 'fair test' and conduct an enquiry in the domain of physical sciences in the primary school, greater emphasis on oral and written communication in modern language teaching, pupils negotiating their curriculum in prevocational courses, basing remedial reading programmes on effective diagnosis of needs and difficulties, and many others. In each case there is an assumption that teachers may well need to reconstruct, sometimes radically, their favoured teaching patterns if they adopt a new curriculum.

Each of the developments described above may need little change from some teachers, as they may already foster enquiry or engage in extensive oral communication, but others may need to change dramatically what they do. All such strategies and programmes, should they be novel to a particular teacher, presuppose a significant shift in classroom behaviour. Instead of telling pupils, the teacher may have to set up conditions under which they can find out for themselves. Equally the obverse may apply and the teacher may need to impart more information than previously. In the case of any curriculum which is negotiated rather than imposed, both teacher and pupil may need to act more flexibly and responsively to each other. In looking critically at the curriculum in a school there are two elements that lend themselves to classroom observation, namely *implementation* and *evaluation*.

Implementation

The simple questions in the case of implementation studies are: 'Is the teacher doing what the curriculum developers intended?' and 'Is the teacher doing what she herself intended?' In this context classroom observation can be used to match *intent* against *action*. However, it must be made clear from the outset that this should not be used as a repressive measure. Teachers should be able to use their imagination, not be expected to act as clones of some curriculum developer who never comes near their own classroom. The purpose of looking at implementation is to see whether there is a mismatch between intention and strategies. Someone seeking to improve pupils' competence in speaking a foreign language might be expected to encourage them to use the target language in the classroom. If observation showed that there were hardly any opportunities to use or listen to the language being learned, then this would be something that could be brought to the teacher's attention.

The first stage of looking at implementation is for the teachers concerned to discuss the new curriculum and consider what changes in practice might be required. The next stage is to draw up some agreed form of observation, so that an observer, who might well be a fellow teacher, or a deputy head responsible for curriculum development and implementation, has a clear idea of what to look for. Finally there can be a discussion of what has been found. Suppose, for example, there is a curriculum policy that children should learn to conduct their own enquiries in science lessons. The process might involve:

1   Teachers looking at the outline of the curriculum to see what kinds of topics and activities might be devised with children of different ages to foster scientific enquiry, for example: devising a fair test to find out which of a tennis ball, a table tennis ball and a ball made of clay will bounce higher; hypothesising what will happen if you pass an electric current through more than one light bulb; working out how much energy people or machines need to carry out their work.

2   An observation outline is drawn up, concentrating on the opportunities teachers give children to devise experiments, what the teacher actually does during the lesson, how the six target pupils conduct themselves, followed by

a brief interview proforma, or questionnaire to see how teacher and pupils viewed the process.

3   A deputy head responsible for curriculum observes lessons, assisted by other teachers or student teachers on an occasional basis.

4   Staff discussion of what has been found.

Skilfully handled, this can raise many professional issues and offer teachers feedback about the actuality of the initiative. There is always the important issue to consider, however, of how this will be received by the teachers concerned. If it is seen as pressure by the more powerful people in the school to ensure conformity to a single party line on teaching, then there may well be negative repercussions. On the other hand if it is seen as a joint effort to scrutinise, reflect on and amend practice in the light of intelligent feedback, then it becomes a different matter, a source of enthusiasm, not resentment. There should always be room for dissent, for some teachers may argue that they feel uncomfortable teaching the 'new' approach. One answer might be to try it, on the grounds that no doubt doctors used to feel some anxiety about giving up leeches as a standard cure for many ills. If after a wholehearted attempt to make something work a teacher still feels uncomfortable, then the school must decide whether it wants all to teach along similar lines or can tolerate diversity.

It is also important to remember that an implementation study can also consider the extent to which teachers are meeting their *own* objectives. If someone intends to go round the class monitoring children's work, but then finds that she is

Figure 4.4 Pupils enquiring in science

marooned at her desk for most of the time, simply giving out word spellings to children who come and ask, then an implementation observation might reveal that she was not able to meet her own principal objective. Subsequent reflection might then come up with proposals that she should spend some time showing children how to use a simple dictionary, so that she could then devote more time to monitoring their other work.

Evaluation

Curriculum evaluation involves a step beyond implementation, for instead of merely looking at whether teachers meet their own or anyone else's intention, the focus is on how effectively the curriculum, in both its theoretical and actual form, allows children to learn. In this context observation can highlight how effective the curriculum is, using a mixture of professional judgement and systematic testing if necessary.

Suppose a school has devoted a great deal of time to discussing communication and information technology, on the grounds that it is an important field and there has been a significant investment in computers, word processors and interactive technology. The following ingredients might be part of an evaluation package:

1   Observation of lessons to see which teachers make use of the classroom technology available, what kinds of activities take place, whether most children have a turn at some time, whether they seem to be positively or negatively disposed towards information technology. Use may be made of target pupils and a pupil pursuit, visiting lessons when it is known that information technology will be used.
2   Observation of lessons where information technology is not used, to see what opportunities might be made available.
3   Interviews with teachers and pupils to elicit their views and experiences.
4   A simple test of proficiency related to the content and objectives of the courses using information technology, of the 'Can do' type, such as 'Can the pupil (a) use a database, (b) type a draft of a document and then try to improve it?' and other similar questions.
5   Discussion of the outcome and consideration of future policy and practice.

Curriculum evaluation can be time consuming, but even if a school targets only one aspect a year to investigate systematically, using whatever time and resources are available, it is a worthwhile investment of energy.

Job analysis

From time to time it is necessary to look at the actual and full job of teaching by analysing the teacher's day. This often reveals that, in addition to classroom interaction between teacher and pupils, there are many hours of activity related to teaching, like preparation and planning, assessment, meeting parents, attending meetings or courses, supervising the playground, attending assembly, marking registers, collecting money, setting out and clearing away. Part of any scrutiny of the teacher's day could involve watching someone at work in the classroom as well. If a school were considering spending some of its money on hiring a classroom assistant, for example, then observation of lessons and interviews with the teachers concerned might reveal aspects of the job which could be done by an assistant. Most dentists do not mix their own filling compounds: they hire a less well qualified person to do that, but not to carry out the highly skilled work.

This is an example of a job analysis with a specific purpose, namely to elicit which part of the classroom work of the teacher might be done by someone with some degree of relevant skills, but not with the full set required by teachers. When the purpose of job analysis is as specific and targeted as this, then the observation methodology can be created to fit the aim. A freehand observation might simply involve noting down points in the lesson at which a classroom assistant would have been useful. Alternatively a time line or checklist might be used. A list of tasks suitable for a classroom assistant could be drawn up. In the case of a class of young children this might involve such items as 'help with clothing' (e.g. dressing at the end of the day), 'social talk', 'collecting and distributing', 'clearing away', 'simple spellings', 'reading story to small group' and so on. Either a time line or a tick list could then be assembled, and the observer would record time spent on each task on graph paper, or check each item when it was noted. This information could then be useful in helping decide how to make best use of a classroom assistant and what kind of person to seek.

Time line
help with clothing   __   _____
social talk   __   __   __   _____
collecting/distributing   __   __   __
Checklist
clearing away   *////*
simple spelling   *///////////////////*
reading story   */*

A job analysis may not always be conducted for a specific reason. Sometimes it is valuable in its own right to know how people spend their time, even if there is no immediate pressure to do anything about it. Observation is only one part of a job analysis, which might also contain self reports and questionnaires or interviews. When under scrutiny people often behave differently, and diaries or logs of work done are notorious for appearing to be inflated, partly because respondents may be under pressure to exaggerate their burden, or because they simply do more work when keeping an account of it.

On the other hand it is important to audit from time to time what teachers are actually doing during their day, even if there are difficulties attached to the exercise, and looking at time spent in the classroom is only one part of that process. Larger scale studies of the nature of teaching may start with observation of teachers both in and out of the classroom. Interviews and observations can reveal a very wide range of tasks performed in a single day, which might include external liaison, such as corresponding with publishers, examination boards, the local authority, the police, social services, as well as internal administration involving governors, finances, ordering goods, and several other matters.

Some studies, like that by Youngman (1984), have assembled large checklists of hundreds of tasks of this kind and then asked different teachers to complete them. This then assembles a picture of not only how teachers spend their time, but also which teachers do what jobs. Youngman studied senior teachers, junior teachers, probationers and trainees in secondary schools, and one of the conclusions from his study was that student teachers were not always invited to attend staff meetings or take a tutor group, yet teachers in their first year often did both these.

Analysis of different people's actual day allows many conclusions of this kind to be reached, and this can be helpful in the planning of training and retraining courses, as well as in making decisions about the sensible deployment of teachers themselves. Observation can reveal that it is not always the case that administration is done solely by the head or the deputy, for example, as other teachers are

'Teaching can be busy'

Figure 4.5 Job analysis

responsible for the children and the materials in their own classroom or home area, and often have to keep records of progress, use of materials, or other aspects of classroom life. It might also reveal not only how much time teachers spend on assessment, but also detailed information about the actual nature of it. This can be particularly important if it involves elaborate one-to-one testing, as it can with younger children, or the administering of practical tests and other labour-intensive forms of assessment, where time must be used wisely

Teacher appraisal

The formal appraisal of teachers usually requires at least some consideration of what they actually do in the classroom, rather than just a broad assessment of the generalities of their work. If appraisal is seen as nothing more than a legally required ritual that has to be enacted at intervals through clenched teeth, then the classroom observation part of it will be perfunctory and apologetic. But if it is regarded as a sustained process, an essential part of professional life, not an unwelcome addition to it, then the appraisal of what happens in the classroom, especially self-appraisal, is an important element of keeping the school under review. When we studied over 1,000 teachers who had taken part in the first cycle of compulsory appraisal of teachers (Wragg et al.. 1996), we found that some 28 per cent of teachers had been observed on only one occasion, even though a minimum of two observations had been the official requirement. Some schools simply did not give it a high priority.

In order to make an impact, any formal appraisal of teaching competence must be both retrospective and prospective, looking back at what has been achieved and forward to what might be done in the future. Furthermore the commitment of the teachers concerned to improving individual and collective classroom practice must be secured, otherwise changes for the better are unlikely. An observer can sit in and watch only on an occasional basis, whereas teachers themselves will teach thousands of lessons in a relatively short period of their career. If appraisal is meant to improve the quality of teaching, then real long-lasting changes in teaching styles are better than cosmetic changes staged to please an observer.

Several questions need answering before an appraisal exercise is undertaken. These include:

1 What is the principal purpose of the exercise?
2 Who will observe whom and what will the focus be?
3 What kind of preparation will be necessary (training of observers, briefing of teachers)?
4 Under what conditions should observations take place (how often, on what days, with which classes or groups)?
5 What format will be used (freehand note taking, checklist, semi-structured schedule)?
6 By whom and according to what principles will the format be devised?

7   What form of debriefing and discussion will take place after observations?
8   What record of the appraisal will be kept and who will have access to it?
9   What targets will be set for the future?
10   What will be done to support teachers seeking to improve what they do as a result of appraisal, and how will the achieving of targets be monitored?

The most common form of classroom appraisal is the *superior-subordinate* model, whereby a more senior person looks at the teaching of someone of more junior standing. Yet *peer appraisal*, which involves two people of equal rank watching each other teach, can also be a valuable exercise, if properly conceived, and various suggestions for that have been made earlier in this book. The appraisal of classroom competence will be most effective if improving teaching is a central part of the school's professional culture, not something grafted on at widely separated intervals, and peer appraisal is a good way of focusing on the importance to every teacher of mutually supportive critical reflection and a commitment to positive action. The matter of appraisal will be discussed again in Chapter 6.

Performance criteria

The notion of 'performance' sits uneasily in many teachers' vocabulary, for the word is more commonly associated with circus animals, entertainment and a mechanical view of industrial and commercial enterprise. For those who see teaching as an art, or as a process requiring a variety of professional skills that are not always instantly demonstrable (it is not easy to stage, to order, a show of 'encouraging slower learners' or 'dealing with difficult adolescents'), the word 'performance' will not do. However, notions such as 'performance-related pay' often occur in discourse about teaching, as do terms such as 'performance-based' or 'competency-based' teacher education.

If the word 'performance' cannot be dry cleaned of its mechanical and financial associations, then it is perhaps better simply to think of teachers improving the quality of what they do over a period of time, and whether written criteria are helpful. If it is useful to write down what are thought to be the elements of skilful teaching, then the next possibility is that these might be written in the form of a *hierarchy of levels*, that is conceived in such a way that a teacher can see a line of development or progression. Thus level 1 might be the sort of simple level achieved by a beginner early on a first teaching practice, whereas level 10 would be the aspiration of the very experienced master teacher.

Harvard and Dunne (1992) have described how trainees can assess themselves and be assessed on a set of nine dimensions. These include 'direct instruction', 'monitoring', 'management of order' and 'planning and preparation'. In each case, there are eight levels through which teachers can progress, level 1 being what is expected of beginners and level 8 being the mark of a competent practitioner. Some examples are as follows:

Level 1

1 Distribute provided materials: check children's responses.
2 Attempt to operate some procedures for orderly activity.
3 Plan basis resources for children working on a given activity.
4 Give some account of own performance.
5 Check clarity of explanation by appropriate questions: convey enthusiasm with appropriate verbal and non-verbal behaviour.
6 Use planned and unplanned opportunities to hold conversations with children in order to establish their perspectives, be sensitive to problems of teacher intrusion.
7 Continue with attempts to operate in an established formula of rules and procedures.

Level 5

1 Provide a programme of guided practice in core areas of the curriculum to suit range of attainments in class: choose appropriately matched and sequenced practice exercises.
2 Experiment with planned conversational teaching on particular aspects of the curriculum.
3 Plan a short programme of work to engage a variety of identified skills and intellectual processes and demonstrate attention to transition between activities.
4 Offer justifiable explanations of children's response to work: use explanations in practicable ways to plan the next phase of work and show understanding of the diversity of pupils' attainments.

Level 8

1 Make explanations efficient and concise: choose examples for their power in the subject.
2 Sustain a broad programme of diagnostic teaching.
3 Achieve a situation in which order is endemic to the work system.
4 Plan for efficiency in use of time and resources with clear reference to the careful management of the teacher's time.

There are several problems with a hierarchical view of competence, despite its obvious appeal as a clearly drawn ladder of development. One is that the highest levels can be such that even gifted teachers may pale at the thought of trying to achieve them, and all of us feel guilty when we do not attain them. Another is that the nature of the levels, despite the apparent precision, can still be vague and diffuse, using words like 'adequate' or 'considerable' that are open to widely differing interpretations. A third difficulty occurs when some powerful person draws up a hierarchy which people are then obliged to meet if they wish to receive a favourable appraisal or qualify for higher pay. Nonetheless, such a mapping exercise can help clarify what people might aspire to, and the Exeter model is offered as an example, not as a paragon ideal to be copied. It is often more effective if a group of teachers work out a set of classroom appraisal precepts to which they feel committed personally and professionally, than if one is merely imposed on them.

Incompetent teachers

Formal appraisal is sometimes linked with, sometimes divorced from disciplinary action against teachers judged to be incompetent. In some countries the annual or biennial appraisal of classroom competence is a time when those judged to be unsatisfactory can be warned or even dismissed. In other countries there is a deliberate distancing between formal appraisal and rewards or retribution. Whichever approach to appraisal is adopted, some judgements about incompetence are bound to be made or confirmed whenever thousands of teachers are observed at work in their classrooms, even if the general conclusion is that the vast majority are competent.

When we undertook the Teaching Competence Project at Exeter University (Wragg 1997), it was the first large-scale British study that had addressed the issue of incompetent teachers, partly because it is a sensitive matter, and partly because it is difficult to arrive at a teacher's class saying, 'I'm doing a study of incompetent teachers and the head has given me your name …'. In one of the few published reports on the topic, Bridges (1986) looked at 141 school districts in California and concluded that incompetence was of many kinds and occurred for several reasons. Few teachers judged to be poor at their work fell down on only one criterion. Incompetence, like competence, is not unidimensional. It may include failing to keep order, not knowing or being able to impart subject matter effectively, inability to accept advice about improvement, treat the children properly or achieve a reasonable standard of work from them. Often several of these may be noted in the same teacher.

Bridges found that incompetence could be extremely consuming of both time and money, with high legal costs for dismissals, a great deal of time, especially from senior people, extensive documentation and considerable frustration when little seemed to be done. Heads of schools often preferred to accommodate, rather than to dismiss, because of all the legal and administrative difficulties, so they rearranged timetables to minimise the damage to one class, or assigned teachers to non-teaching duties. Some tried to secure the 'induced exit', which involved bombarding incompetent teachers with every complaint received from parents or fellow teachers until they left.

One of the most difficult problems occurred with teachers who were generally incompetent, but who were able to stage a satisfactory lesson when they were observed. If observation is part of the procedure for coping with incompetence, then there need to be several observations, not just one or two, otherwise those who can wheel out a single bright idea when visited may appear to be satisfactory when they are not. In any case there is more to dealing with incompetence than making a single visit. Most teachers who are not doing as well as they should, may well have other personal problems to do with their health, relationships or their life outside school. Concentrating solely on what happens inside the classroom may ignore the underlying causes of incompetence.

Dismissal may be the only solution in the end, if all else fails, but along the way there is a long process of informal and formal warnings, counselling, spelling out what it is the teacher is not doing well and areas where improvements can be made, drawing up a specific and written set of targets, giving opportunities to attend courses or work at classroom competence in other ways. Classroom observation by a skilled person can be a useful part of this process, and there are many examples of teachers who fell on hard times but were helped back by someone who saw them teach and made suggestions, as well as some, sadly, who appeared immune to all offers of help. Dealing with allegations of incompetence is another matter that will be dealt with again in Chapter 6.

Observation by lay people

From time to time the issue is raised as to whether there is a place in the classroom for people who have a legitimate interest in a school, perhaps as parents, governors, supporters or sponsors, but who are not themselves professionally trained as teachers. The question that is asked is either a general one, like: 'Should lay people ever observe lessons?', or a very specific one, such as: 'Should school governors take part in teacher appraisal by observing lessons?' Lay people are part of school inspection teams in the United Kingdom.

My own view is very simple, so it is worth stating explicitly. Lay people such as parents and governors, or others who are trying to support the school and its community, have a perfect right to see what is happening in the classroom, but should not be involved in such matters as the appraisal of teaching competence. Whatever intuitive insights they may apply when looking at teaching, these should not feature in appraisal. That is a professional matter. However, many schools encourage legitimate visitors to the classroom, provided they can accommodate them and still get on with their teaching, and there are several ways in which outsiders who do not normally have access to classrooms can observe teaching. These include:

1 Having an open day when visitors may enter any classroom and watch what is going on (proper arrangements need to be made to avoid over-crowding).

2 Arranging the hall in the evening so that half of it is set out like a classroom and the other half contains chairs for the audience. A maths, English or modern language lesson can then be staged, with the teacher and a class trying

to simulate what they would normally do, and the audience able to ask questions afterwards.

3   Showing a video of one or more classrooms and explaining to the audience the nature of the activities.

4   Inviting parents into the classroom in the evening and then putting on a lesson of the kind their children have had during the day, say a science lesson or a project, so that they can see and discuss what their children do in class.

A few years ago I was involved in a home and school project in which schools explored such ways of giving parents the feel of what happened in lessons. Some teachers were apprehensive about being seen at work, but interviews with parents showed they were both impressed by what they had seen and grateful for the opportunity to penetrate what had previously seemed a complete mystery. There is obviously a danger that what is seen in such circumstances is a distortion of real classroom life, that teachers or pupils may show off, be on their guard, or do something unusual merely to impress. That may be a hazard worth coping with if the alternative, of not seeing what goes on at all, is thought to be worse. In the situations described, it is probably wisest to let parents or other visitors observe the process in a natural way, rather than burden them with structured schedules or other paraphernalia, but short notes of guidance, explaining what the teacher is trying to achieve and how it fits in with other work, can be helpful.

Chapter 5

Research into classrooms

Very little money is spent on research into education generally and into classroom teaching in particular. This is in stark contrast with what is done in other fields, where research and development are seen as vital components if the industry is to thrive. Many industrial and commercial concerns, particularly in a field like the pharmaceutical or defence industry, invest a significant percentage of their profits in research and development work in order to survive and compete. Parts of the American pharmaceutical industry invest 20 per cent of their profits in research, yet in education less than one-thousandth of the multi-billion dollar investment is spent on research (Biddle 1989). Indeed, most of the research in education nowadays is done by individuals, many of whom are studying for some kind of qualification, often higher degrees on a part-time basis, rather than by large-scale externally funded project teams. Of the relatively small sum spent on educational research, a great deal goes on such matters as pupil assessment. Very little cash is donated to studies of teachers at work in their own classrooms.

There is also widespread cynicism about the purpose and impact of educational research, even within the teaching profession. Yet classroom observation research can make a significant contribution to the improvement of teaching competence, especially if teachers and schools, as a matter of policy, research their own practice and act on their findings. Rosenshine and Furst (1973) proposed a *descriptive-correlational-experimental loop* model, which would involve first of all description of what happens in classrooms, then a systematic study of the correlation between process and outcome, and finally experiments to see if the correlational findings were an artefact. Many researchers since have explored variations of the theme that what are often tentative research findings should be tested out in the classroom, and indeed that teachers should effectively be action researchers.

For example, a descriptive study of classroom processes based on live observation of lessons might describe the way that teachers address questions to children. A correlational study might find a positive link between the teacher calling on pupils by name and measures of pupil learning. However, a correlation does not by itself establish a cause. The province of Burgenland in eastern Austria has sometimes had the highest birthrate in the country. It also happens to be the province with the largest population of storks, but the coincidence of these two factors does not mean that the one causes the other.

In order to establish cause there need to be controlled experiments, Rosenshine and Furst argued, so the investigator of teachers' questions might finally set up experiments in which teachers sometimes call on pupils by name to answer questions, and on other occasions nominate only those whose hands are raised. The outcome would then, in theory at any rate, indicate whether calling on named pupils led to more effective teaching and learning. The problem with this view is first of all that experiments in teaching can often be artificial and difficult to conduct. Whereas in research in the physical sciences it is easy to keep some elements under the direct and precise control of the investigator and specify what temperature or pressure will be maintained, the same certainties cannot be built into classroom research.

If an investigator wished teachers to give pupils information according to a prearranged formula or scripted text, for example, any neat design would immediately be wrecked once a pupil made a spontaneous observation, or asked the teacher a question. At that point, either natural forces would take over and subvert the experiment, or the teacher would ignore any attempt by pupils to make a spontaneous contribution, thereby rendering the experiment meaningless in terms of real classroom life. Most studies of classrooms, therefore, look at teaching in its natural state. In practice true experiments are rare, and *quasi-experimental design*, which looks like an experiment but is not, usually because the groups of pupils involved are not or cannot be matched, is much more common. It is frequently the case that observation studies do not involve any kind of experiment at all. Someone studying the teaching of reading by different methods is more likely to compare teachers who already prefer one approach or another, rather than set up an experiment which may appear artificial.

A second problem is that most research into classroom processes tends to reveal only small relationships between process and outcome. A great deal of the research which has compared two methods of teaching has revealed no *general* difference between the two, because different teachers are able to make various methods work effectively if they believe in them, or fail miserably if they do not. Other research has shown only slight differences amounting to one or two percentage points. Gage (1978) felt confident enough, however, even on the basis of small differences identified in the research on teaching styles and pupil learning, to propose a set of 'Teacher should' statements like 'Teachers should keep to a minimum such activities as giving directions and organising the class for instruction' or 'During reading-group instruction, teachers should give a maximal amount of brief feedback and provide fast-paced activities of the "drill" type'.

In his book *Hard Gains in the Soft Sciences*, Gage (1985) counters the criticisms about small differences between experimental and control groups, or low levels of significance, by quoting fields such as medicine and public health, where big changes in policy can be made on the basis of a degree of statistical 'superiority' that would receive scant attention in education. He quotes examples of trials of beta blockers and low cholesterol diets to reduce the incidence of heart attacks. The two sets of trial treatments showed only 2.5 and 1.7 per cent differences respectively between the mortality rates of the experimental and control groups, but the United States government terminated the research and implemented the findings immediately, on the grounds that even small percentages meant that thousands of lives could be saved and it was not worth waiting any longer if some unnecessary deaths would occur in the mean time. Yet if an educational researcher discovered a 2.5 or 1.7 per cent superiority of one method over another in the teaching of algebra, it is highly unlikely that much notice would be taken.

Research questions

Despite the difficulties of conducting rigorous research into classroom processes it is nonetheless well worth making the attempt. In the case of larger scale projects, research into classrooms needs to be seen as adding a thin layer to what was previously known, rather than finding a miracle cure for some particular ill, or embarking on a quest for the philosopher's stone that would turn all to gold. Smaller projects, particularly those done by teachers and heads in their own school, can make a valuable impact on local practice. If there were a modest but enthusiastic research ethos in every school, not only would the quality of teaching and learning stand a good chance of improving significantly, but an important message would be transmitted from teachers to pupils, namely: 'We expect you to have an enquiring mind because we ourselves do'

Twenty questions about the classroom

In the field of classroom processes numerous research questions present themselves. These include the following twenty, by no means an exhaustive list, merely a few illustrative examples from a vast reservoir of possibilities:

1 What do teachers and pupils do in the classroom; how do they spend their time?
2 What kind of interaction takes place, who talks to whom and about what?
3 How do teachers manage their classes; what are the classroom rules; how are elements such as time, space, pupil behaviour, or their own teaching strategies managed?
4 What do pupils learn; what tasks do they engage in, and with what degree of involvement and success?
5 What is a school day or a lesson like from a pupil's point of view; are any individuals or groups getting a relatively poor deal out of schooling?
6 What happens to particularly able pupils or those with learning difficulties?
7 How are different subjects/topics taught to different age groups?
8 What happens in the classroom when there is a change of policy, a new curriculum, work scheme, textbook course, or new forms of assessment?

9   How are classroom decisions made, by the teacher, by pupils, by both in negotiation?
10 What happens when pupils disrupt lessons or behave in an anti-social manner?
11 How can I improve my own teaching?
12 Is there continuity and coherence in the curriculum, or does it appear disjointed and incoherent from the child's point of view?
13 Do teachers in the same school or department have similar or different practices, beliefs, expectations, rewards and punishments, conventions, and how are these understood by the pupils?
14 Do teachers and children perceive the same events in different or similar ways?
15 What happens when a child does not understand something?
16 How do teachers explain new topics to pupils?
17 How is pupils' work monitored and assessed in the classroom?
18 What happens when children work in small groups; what sort of assignments are undertaken; who decides what; are the groups collaborative?
19 What is the place of subject knowledge; what knowledge, skills, attitudes and behaviour seem to be acquired; what happens if the teacher does not know the factual detail of a particular piece of subject matter?
20 How do teachers make their classroom decisions?

Some of these research questions are more straightforward than others, and often the questions which most interest teachers or administrators are not necessarily those that attract research projects, hence the importance of teachers' research into their own practice. 'How can I improve my own practice?' or 'Do some individuals and groups get a relatively poor deal out of schooling?' are legitimate questions, but are not immediately translatable into research terms. For research purposes one of the first priorities is to establish greater clarity about the meaning of words like 'improve' or 'poor', for these would be differently understood and interpreted by different people.

On a day-to-day basis it is perfectly possible to make personal and professional judgements about such questions, and we could not function if we did not do so, as the hundreds of events in which teachers and pupils are engaged every day cannot wait for a fully fledged research project to report. However, when time is taken to mount a proper enquiry, then it is worth taking the trouble to define the purpose, focus and intention of it, before embarking on a series of lesson observations. There are numerous other questions about classroom processes that can be asked, and many of the ones stated above can be the focus of what is sometimes called a 'quick and dirty' piece of *ad hoc* enquiry, using occasional classroom observation, or it can become a lifetime's study.

Training observers

If the findings of observers are to be credible then they must receive training, or at least have the opportunity to discuss their purposes, procedures and intentions to the point where there is general agreement on what they will be doing. If a research project is using mainly qualitative methodology, then the researchers need to agree what questions are to be addressed, how they will collect data, whether they will make notes or operate to some other agreed procedures, and how their findings will be analysed and reported. It is particularly important that the main focus of the investigation is known, as books full of notes on lessons, or sound and video recordings, can soon proliferate to the point where they defy analysis.

Once this is clear then training can involve analysis and discussion of lesson transcripts, observation of videos and visits to actual lessons, with observers talking through what they see until there is some agreement about the way in which events will be scrutinised and the form in which records will be assembled. One way of doing this is known as *triangulation*, a process analogous to that used by surveyors, who draw a triangle on a map and then take measurements that can then be related to each other at each of the three corners.

Triangulation in classroom research involves checking the perceptions of more than one person to see if one's own interpretations have any support. This might involve talking to fellow observers, teachers, pupils, where this is agreed, as well as other forms of record, like documents and accounts of meetings. Thus if a teacher rewarded a child for getting full marks in a test and said that this had been made school policy recently, that all children knew about it and were in favour of it, the observer could study other events, interview participants, and look at policy documents and minutes of meetings to refute or verify what had been said.

Denzin (1985) distinguishes four different kinds of triangulation:

1   *data triangulation* involving different time, space or people
2   *investigator triangulation* where various observers cross-check each other
3   *theory triangulation* which brings different theories to bear on the observations
4   *methodological triangulation* whereby more than one methodology of enquiry is employed.

In all of these approaches both the similarities and differences between the perceptions of various participants and observers or methods of enquiry are of interest.

When a category system or checklist is employed then the procedure is similar, except that it is necessary to make a formal quantified check of how much agreement there is between observers. This can be done in many ways, depending on how complex the system is. Training can begin with observers learning the category system and then applying it to a transcript of a lesson and discussing their assignment of events to categories. For example, if they are using a category system to code teachers' questions, they would need to decide whether a question like, 'Is a duck a mammal?' would count as a simple closed information recall question, since 'No' is the only correct textbook answer, or as something of a slightly higher order, if the teacher's tone and manner appear to be inviting the child to explain why, and give a 'No, because …' answer.

(a) observer's view

(c) pupil's view

(b) teacher's view

Figure 5.1 Triangulation (a) observer's view (b) teacher's view (c) pupil's view

There are two formal measures of agreement between observers when more than one person is involved:

1 *inter-observer agreement* the amount of agreement between two or more observers
2 *intra-observer agreement* the extent to which observers agree with themselves.

Usually the same videotape of a classroom is used before and after the observation part of the project. This allows observers to compare their first coding of it with their second coding some time later, thus showing both types of agreement, or lack of it: between different observers, and between the same observers on different occasions. The type of comparison depends on the nature of the quantitative data being collected. If rating scales were being used, then a correlation between the first and second set of ratings might be appropriate.

If a category system is being employed, then the simplest check would be the percentage of agreement on each person's tallies of the same events. To do this you simply count up all the occasions when observers agree and all the ones when they disagree. Thus they might agree on 82 per cent of their codings and disagree on 18 per cent. This figure would then be reported in the research account so that the reader knows how reliable the data are. If there is less than about 70 per cent agreement, then some caution would have to be exercised in interpreting the results. If the category system had numerous categories that never occurred (like 'teacher flies round room' or 'pupil pole vaults through window'), then it would be easy to obtain high agreement figures because of the many empty cells, but most category systems are not as comically unrealistic as this.

Two observers might obtain the following results, based on the analysis of the same videotaped lessons before and after the project, and then calculating the extent to which they agree with each other and themselves:

Inter-observer agreement		Percentage agreement
Beginning of project	(Observer A with Observer B)	82
End of project	(Observer A with Observer B)	78
Intra-observer agreement		
Observer A (beginning of project) with self (end of project)		84
Observer B (beginning of project) with self (end of project)		71

This would tell the reader that there was fairly high agreement between the two observers at the beginning of the project, a little less at the end, and that Observer A showed greater stability in coding over time (84 per cent agreement) than Observer B (71 per cent).

Some researchers use a chi square to compare distributions, and Flanders (1970) used Darwin's chi square, a variation of the normal chi square, which has been modified to recognise that communication events are not independent of each other (for example, a pupil's answer is more likely to follow a teacher's question than occur randomly). The main point about training, however, is to secure agreement about principles and practice, clarity about purpose and actions, and to give time for different observers to discuss any disagreements or sources of confusion.

Research instruments

A description of the various approaches to classroom observation has been given in earlier chapters, but sometimes more than one approach is used in research. Observers may wish to amplify or corroborate their observations with interviews, questionnaires or tests of various kinds.

Interviews

Commonly used to elicit the views of participants, they can be

- *structured* (yes/no, either/or, multiple choice type items, etc.)
- *semi-structured* (written questions asked to each interviewee, but with probes and open ended questions to encourage a certain amount of natural conversation)
- *unstructured* (free-ranging conversation).

Semi-structured interview schedules are often preferred by classroom researchers, as they raise key questions, but also allow the observer and teacher to have some natural conversation about events. A semi-structured interview schedule used to amplify critical events might look like this:

Can you tell me what happened when …? (cue critical event)

What do you think led up to … (critical event)?

What is your own reaction to … (critical event)?

How do you think X and Y (any pupils involved) feel about what happened?

The interviewer is then able to insert probes and prompts as conversation develops. Powney and Watts (1987) have written a useful book on interviewing.

Questionnaires

Questionnaires are overused in research generally, and since the classroom observer is present with the teacher concerned, it is often better to use a structured interview schedule on the spot, rather than leave a questionnaire behind. However, questionnaires can be useful in surveying large numbers of teachers about their classroom practice, an approach used by Bennett (1976) in his study of teaching styles, and by Wragg *et al.* (1996) to discover how appraisers used classroom observation when evaluating fellow teachers. Bennett devised a questionnaire that asked teachers to report whether they gave regular spelling tests, used group work, allowed children to choose their own seat, preferred teaching single subjects or cross-curricular topics, and was then able to compare profiles and draw up a series of clusters of teachers with similar preferred styles. Questionnaires allow teachers the time to give a considered reply to questions, and also permit the researcher to select a sample of teachers with differing or perhaps similar accounts of preferred practice, and then observe them at work in their own classroom. The major disadvantage is that mailed questionnaires, especially if teachers are busy, can have a notoriously low return rate, below 10 per cent being quite common. Oppenheim (1992) has written a comprehensive text on the construction of questionnaires and attitude measures.

Tests

The number of tests on the market is now so enormous that huge textbooks and catalogues have to be compiled even to display a relatively small selection of them. Classroom researchers might use tests of attitude, personality, subject knowledge, or another focus such as self-concept. Possibilities include studying the relationship between teacher attributes and classroom behaviour ('Do introvert and extravert teachers behave differently?', 'What relationship is there between stated attitude towards innovation and actual implementation of it?'). A common use of testing is to see what pupils have learned, or how their attitudes have changed, often known as *process–product research.* This was a popular approach in the 1970s and 1980s, when Eggleston, *et al.* (1975) used tests of both attitude and learning in their observation study of science lessons in order to see how children reacted to different styles of teaching. They found that poor achievement and attitude were associated with lessons which were largely theoretical in approach and which involved little or no practical work.

There are many other research techniques that can be employed, such as the repertory grid developed by Kelly (1955), which allows qualitative researchers to elicit children's or teacher's constructs by presenting them with three names of fellow pupils or teachers, and then asking them to describe ways in which two of them are different from the third. This permits the investigator to assemble a picture of each person's individual construction of the world and then compare it with what happens in the classroom. This approach was used by Nash (1973) who found that pupils had a clear idea of their own and others' relative achievement in reading and mathematics, even though their teachers thought that they did not. Wragg *et al.* (1998) also found that children were able to read various classroom cues to make judgements about their own proficiency in reading. Cohen (1976) has described numerous tests and other instruments for use in classroom research, and Keeves (1988) has brought together a collection of articles on different research instruments that would be useful to investigators. The best advice to classroom researchers, however, is to start with the questions, not the instruments. Choice of tools should come after the relevant questions have been formulated and purposes and intentions clarified.

Language in the classroom

The study of language in the classroom is so labour intensive that it is much less common than other forms of classroom interaction research. It is, however, a focus of scrutiny favoured by qualitative researchers, sometimes as a topic for investigation in its own right, sometimes as a source for making inferences about the significance, intention and meaning which lie beneath events. Malinowski (1922), the anthropologist whose pioneering studies of Trobriand Islanders have been influential on participant observers in other domains, advocated assembling a 'synoptic record', a collection of statements from informants, which could form a basis for making inferences about the structure and purposes of behaviour.

It is one thing to have a collection of transcripts, lesson protocols or interview statements, but quite another to know how best to analyse these. Some of the researchers into classroom language have not been people with a background in education, but rather in linguistics. Sinclair and Coulthard (1975), who worked in a university English department, found classroom discourse a fascinating subject to study in its own right: 'We ... wanted a situation where all participants were genuinely trying to communicate and where potentially ambiguous utterances were likely to have one accepted meaning'.

They found just that kind of situation in the classrooms they studied. Their analysis was divided into several ranks, beginning with *lessons*, then *transactions*; within these were *exchanges*, which in turn enclosed *moves*, which eventually zoomed in on specific *acts*. They found that teachers frequently had to structure not only the relevant knowledge, but also the form in which it was to be purveyed. This frequently produced meta-statements, that is statements about the process itself, like 'Let's see who understands what I've just been explaining'. The 'moves' included opening something up ('Suppose ...'), focusing ('Look at this picture and see if ...') and following up ('That's right').

Detailed linguistic analysis of transcripts often results in insights that can easily be missed in the rapid exchanges of classroom interaction, like the identification by Barnes *et al.* (1967) of questions that were genuinely open and those that were 'pseudo-open', that is, appeared on the surface to be inviting a wide range of possible responses, but in reality sought just the one preferred by the teacher. In these circumstances pupils frequently realise the kind of guessing game involved and scan the teacher's facial and linguistic responses to help them grope towards the approved reply.

Some analysts of transcripts prefer to read them through carefully and pick out key concepts or notions using a highlighter pen, or extracting relevant quotes on to large sheets of paper under different headings. Thus a researcher studying teachers' reactions to pupils' answers might pull out examples of 'reinforcement' ('Good', 'Well done'), 'criticism' ('No, you fool', 'You've not been listening to what I've been saying'), 'enhancement' ('Yes, quite right, and what's more…', 'Now John's just told us that we're going to need warm clothes, and the reason for that is …'), or 'switching' ('No Susan … Melanie, you have a try').

Analysis by computer is often used to cope with large numbers of transcripts, and a good deal of software is now available for qualitative analysis of speech. There is nothing magical about these packages. The researcher simply invents a coding system, or uses an existing one, and then attaches the relevant coding to each segment of text. A set of terms like 'diagnosis', 'response', 'reprimand', 'opening' or 'closure' may be used. It is possible for segments to overlap, and most programs have other flexible features, allowing the researcher to search for and recall all segments that have been similarly coded. Whole lessons, as well as individual teachers and pupils can also be given codes, allowing the investigator to compare instances involving the same people, for example. Computer programs are not a replacement for intelligent analysis, but rather a useful tool for those doing a lot of it.

The classroom is a place where pupils learn and practise a wide variety of forms of expression, some of which are highly stylised exchanges and rarely occur outside education, like the rapid drilling and closed questioning which only happens during schooling and the interrogation of suspects by the police. Other exchanges, however, are valuable rehearsals for life itself, as Edwards and Westgate (1987), advocating the importance of language research in their valuable book on classroom talk, point out:

> Most of our everyday life depends on skills in talking and making sense of the talk of others, as we work or trade or simply pass the time of day. These skills go far beyond the uttering of sounds related to objects, actions or ideas. In our speech we select and organize our utterances according to our sense of what is correct and appropriate in a particular setting. This is partly a matter of grammar, partly of social etiquette, partly of culture, and essentially of assuming that others will be perceiving the same situation as we do.

Action research

One of the most attractive forms of investigation is research and development or *action research* as it is often known. Here the investigator not only observes lessons, but also takes action on the basis of what is witnessed. When it works well, there is a strong feeling that something is being done and that research is more than just documents lying on a library shelf. Action research, because it involves *intervention*, is not especially easy to conduct in a rigorous manner. Investigators may, in the end, be researching themselves and the effectiveness of their own intervention programme, and that can be highly problematic.

There are two principal kinds of action research and classroom observation can have a part to play in both. The first type is largely *rational-reactive*. The investigator looks at what is happening in the classroom, usually with a specific focus on something known to be a problem or in need of improvement, and then draws up a programme to react to, or remediate, what has been discovered. The second type is more *intuitive-proactive*, which means that the researchers or prime movers know, or think they know, what needs to be done, so they implement an intervention programme first, and then visit classrooms to see how well it is progressing.

Rational-reactive research

As an example of action research that is *reactive*, let us suppose that a school in a tough neighbourhood is concerned about the number of pupils involved in rowdy behaviour who are frequently being excluded from the school or contained in some way that is not thought to be satisfactory. The following set of procedures might be followed.

Stage one

Observe lessons to see what kind of disruptive behaviour was occurring. Use a mixture of systematic observation with a schedule of events like 'illicit movement', 'aggression towards fellow pupil', 'altercation with teacher' or 'damage to property', noting down any critical events that occur.

Stage two

Analyse classroom observation data and discover that the problems mainly occurred with pupils aged 13 to 15, that most poor behaviour appeared to result from boredom, lack of or inconsistent application of classroom rules, inappropriate tasks which appeared not to motivate or engage pupils, and that most misbehaviour involved about four or five pupils in each class.

Stage three

Discussion of findings with teachers and, if available, external or internal adviser. Draw up action/intervention programme involving different approach to difficult classes with shorter projects and more practical work, in which the objectives were clearly spelled out, so that pupils could see what they would achieve in a certain time. Teachers discuss with pupils, and if necessary parents, classroom rules that would be enforced, and also recognition of good behaviour. Agreement about consistent ways of handling certain kinds of poor behaviour, and who would take responsibility for what, for example, the role of senior teachers and the deputy head and head of the school.

Stage four

Further classroom observation and interviews to see (a) the extent to which teachers are implementing the agreed programme and (b) what misbehaviour occurs, using the same mixture of structured observation and the noting of critical events as was employed before the new programme started.

Stage five

Evaluate the findings and modify or fine tune the programme as necessary.

Intuitive-proactive research

A *proactive* approach is usually based on some individual's or group's proposal for improvement, often on intuitive grounds. It would follow most of the stages described for reactive research, except that the initial data collection would be different if the progenitors of the idea felt that they already knew what was needed. Curriculum development work is often of this kind, where teachers feel that they know intuitively, from teaching their classes, what needs to be done, so they simply use their imagination to devise a new programme to replace the old one. The research part, therefore, might be largely classroom observation after the innovation to see what happened. In practice the distinction between reactive and proactive action research is often more diffuse than is portrayed here.

Pros and cons

The difficulties with action research projects of any kind are first that they are often conducted by the innovators themselves (and the research literature is heavy with accounts of intervention programmes that are deemed to have 'worked' for their pioneers, but not for the sceptics who tried to replicate them) and with experimental groups that 'beat' control groups. Only rarely does the control group ever 'win' in these circumstances. It is frequently the sheer drive, energy and enthusiasm of the instigators of the programme that are being evaluated, rather than their methods. One way round this compounding of subjectivity is to try and involve an external evaluator or more objective in-house person, who can approach the classroom observation and interview part of the project competently, but with some emotional detachment. Lack of proper resources for action research means that the people and time needed to implement it rigorously are not always available. Yet when done well, action research can be one of the most rewarding and effective means of improving teaching, and investment in it is thoroughly worthwhile.

Research design

The classic research design of an experimental and control group matched in every respect, apart from the experimental component, is not always possible in classroom research. Even two classes thought to be parallel may be sufficiently different in important respects to ruin the experiment. For example, if out of two groups of children who were supposed to be matched for ability and social background, one group happened to contain two particularly disruptive pupils, then any study of a programme to reduce disruptive behaviour would be affected by the influence of the two very badly behaved children. If they happened to be in the control group, the experimental group might be deemed to be a great success, but if they were in the experimental group, then the experiment itself could easily be labelled a failure. Most studies of teaching take place in a naturalistic setting, and the investigator frequently has no control over which pupil is in which class. Even when groups are carefully matched on some criteria, they can be unmatched on others.

Campbell and Stanley (1963) described a series of designs, from the one shot case study to complex models with groups of different kinds. Three designs for classroom observation are shown below. In each case O = observation and/or testing, X = Experiment.

Experimental and control group design

Model A

Group 1 (experimental)	O	X	O
Group 2 (control)	O		O

This is the classic experimental and control group design, observed before and after the experiment. In theory only the experimental 'X' is different, so if the groups are initially matched any changes (test scores, pupil or teacher behaviour, etc.) in the second observation are explained by the effects of the experiment. In practice it is not quite so clear cut, as matching is often less than perfect. Experiments often appear to work largely because of the enthusiasm of the experimenters, the greater attention paid to the subjects, and other influences. The likelihood of any experiment appearing to work positively is often referred to as the *Hawthorne effect* after the research into improving worker performance in the Hawthorne factory of the Western Electrical Company. Output improved under each of the experimental conditions tried by investigators, partly because of the positive response by workers to being shown interest.

Time series of observations

Model B

Group 1	O1	O2	O3	O4	O5	O6	O7	O8
Group 2		O1		O2		O3		O4

This is one of many possible designs for a time series of observations, and different groups may be observed on different occasions to monitor changes over a period of time. Observations can occur at the same times, or on different occasions, to see what, for example, is the effect of the regular presence of an observer, or simply to make best use of the observation time available. Also experimental elements can be introduced between observations, so that their immediate and delayed effects can be monitored.

Four group design

Model C

Group 1 (experimental 1)	O	X	O
Group 2 (control 1)	O		O
Group 3 (experimental 2)		X	O
Group 4 (control 2)			O

This four group design is too elaborate and complex for most observers, but it attempts to discover whether the experiment itself has an effect, or merely the presence of researchers. For example, let us suppose that a researcher is studying the interactions between teachers and pupils of different abilities. The experimental 'X' is a teacher workshop on the teaching of more able and less able children in mixed ability classes. If groups 1 and 3 are different from groups 2 and 4 on the second set of observations, then the changes may be the result of the workshop. If groups 1 and 2 are different from groups 3 and 4, however, then changes may be the result of the teachers changing their behaviour because they have found out after the first visit by observers that interactions with children of high and low ability are being scrutinised, so they may give such pupils more attention on the second set of observations.

Time scales and pilot studies

In practice, since relatively little classroom observation research is based on experiments, most research designs are, in practice, plans of campaign. The investigators decide what forms of observation they will use, what interviews, testing, attitude measures or forms of analysis they will use, with whom and how often. Two valuable steps can be taken by all researchers, whether engaged on national projects, or in small-scale research. The first is to draw up a *time scale*, describing at what point it is intended that each stage of the research should be reached. This can always be modified in the light of experience and actual progress, or lack of it, but at least it is there as a statement of intent.

The second step is to conduct a *pilot study* using exactly the same procedures as will be used in the main study. This is important even if standardised or commonly used procedures are to be employed. It is easy, for experienced researchers as well as beginners, to be over confident about how many lessons they will observe, or how many teachers they will interview. Even observing and interviewing one or two teachers will reveal how feasible the procedures are, how long the process will take and what will be involved in the analysis of the data.

Statistics

It is not possible here to cover the vast array of statistical techniques that have been used in classroom research. In any case, it is important that researchers start with questions, rather than techniques. If an observer wants to know whether the contacts between the teacher and various pupils are significantly different in some way, or if teaching method A leads to more effective learning than teaching method B, then there are probably several statistical approaches, if the data are in quantified form, that might be appropriate. Most of the standard books on statistics for education or the social sciences, like the widely used texts by Guilford (1954) and Kerlinger (1973), cover the common procedures, and in any case, those in doubt should take advice.

Many classroom researchers, especially teachers doing projects for higher degrees or further qualifications, are put off using statistics because of the mystique surrounding them. Some courses on statistics, especially those given by experts unable to empathise with the lay person, are so baffling that participants who start with mental blockages can find these have got worse rather than better. Yet most of the common techniques use little more than multiplication, division, addition and subtraction, or the odd square or square root. The actual mathematics is within the grasp of the average 14 year old, but it is often the pages of formulae with unfamiliar Greek characters like χ or σ, as well as meaningless looking subscripts, that put people off. The most helpful textbooks are frequently the ones with clearly worked examples showing the stages involved.

One problem with classroom observation data is that some unusual distributions can be obtained. Many statistical techniques assume that there is a normal distribution, that is to say that most scores will be around the group's average, or middle of the range of possible scores, with fewer and fewer as one reaches the extremes. Thus on a typical standardised test, most pupils will score in the 40 to 60 per cent range, and very few will get under 5 or over 95 per cent. Classroom observation data can be different. Analysis of teacher talk will find that most teachers speak a great deal, either to the class or to individuals, during a lesson. Rarely does a teacher say nothing. Indeed, having laryngitis necessitates developing a whole new set of teaching strategies for most people, so dependent are we on our voice.

By contrast, a classroom researcher using a schedule with categories like 'teacher uses an analogy', 'pupil strikes teacher' or 'head teacher enters class' may find that these events are much more rare, and in many lessons do not occur at all. Although some forms of classroom event are normally distributed, many are not, and the investigator may need to consider what are known as *non-parametric* or *distribution free statistics*, that is techniques that can deal with rank orders or frequencies, instead of the usual numerical scores. Also, since single or rare events, like the entry of the head or an incident of violent behaviour by a pupil, can have an impact and effect that are far more significant than single instances of more commonplace events, the researcher might in any case be better off using a qualitative approach, rather than the procedures that are more common when there are numerous occurrences.

This is not a statistics textbook, so it is not possible to go into proper detail. Some statistical techniques are simply ways of telling the investigator how likely it is that the results obtained would have occurred by chance, hence the convention of talking about the level of significance in terms of the probability of something occurring by chance being 0.05, 0.01 or 0.001. Since a probability of 1.00 means absolute certainty on 100 per cent of occasions, these three figures simply mean that an event could have occurred by chance in 5 per cent, 1 per cent and 0.1 per cent of cases respectively, in other words with a one in twenty, one in a hundred or one in a thousand likelihood. Sometimes the asterisk convention is also used, with one, two and three asterisks respectively, so that a statistic with a treble asterisk (e.g. $r = 0.76^{***}$) would mean the likelihood of it occurring by chance was one in a thousand. With computers nowadays, it is in any case possible to have the probability calculated to several decimal places, but the three figures above are still used as general indicators.

Many researchers not experienced in statistics often do not know which statistical techniques to look up in the relevant book, and several of the most frequently consulted books contain only a limited repertoire of techniques, ignoring, for example, Bayesian statistics, which considers the probability of an event taking place in the light of other related events. Below are some common needs and a mention of some approaches that, used in proper circumstances, might be appropriate. It must be stressed once more that anyone uncertain should check with a statistician, rather than misuse a procedure.

Relationships between measures

Most commonly, when a relationship is sought between two measures such as amount of misbehaviour and number of pupils applying themselves to the task, a *correlation coefficient* will be used. This ranges from +1 for perfect agreement (the more of one, the more of the other) to –1 for completely inverse relationships (the more of one, the *less* of the other), with zero meaning no relationship. There are many forms of correlation, depending on the nature of the data, Pearson's r being the most common for two sets of continuous measures, like test scores. Two sets of rank orders, or the comparison between a score and a yes/no measure, would involve different forms, such as *Spearman's rho* and *point biserial correlations*.

Comparing groups

This depends on the type of measure involved. If a frequency count has been taken, then a *chi square* might be appropriate. If the occurrence of reprimands in the lessons of teachers in four different age groups were to be compared, then a 'goodness of fit' chi square would look at the distribution actually obtained and compare it with what might have been expected.

When the scores of two groups on something like a rating scale are compared, then if the distribution is roughly normal a *t test* would be appropriate. Suppose the investigator, having rated teachers on a scale from 1 to 10 on some dimension, wanted to see if there was a significant difference between the scores of the male and female teachers, then an *uncorrelated t test* might be used. A *correlated t test* is employed when two sets of scores for the *same* group are compared.

For three or more groups, or for measures that are repeated several times, *analysis of variance* may be used. If scores obtained from watching maths, science and English teachers are subjected to analysis of variance, then the resulting F ratio will reveal whether the differences between all three groups are statistically significant or not. In order to test the significance between any pair of these (say maths and science, or English and maths), a 'gap test' such as *Tukey* or *Scheffé* will be needed. If the distribution of scores is not normal then non-parametric forms of analysis will be needed, like the *Mann-Whitney U* for two groups, and the *Kruskal-Wallis* analysis of variance for three or more groups.

Measuring change

One of the biggest problems in educational research is the measurement of change when groups do not start off equal. Raw unadjusted league tables of schools' test results are an example of the problem of inferring effectiveness from final rather than initial scores. If initial scores are known, then it is possible to calculate what is sometimes known as 'value added'. If two unmatched groups showed the following scores before and after a teaching programme little of note could be deduced about teaching quality:

	Average class test scores	
	Before	After
Group A	35	55
Group B	60	70

We could deduce that the teacher of class B was better than the one who taught class A, because the final test score is higher. We might equally conclude that teacher A must have been better, because class A went up by 20 per cent, and class B by only 10 per cent. That, however, would mean that the teacher of the class that began with a score of zero would almost always look 'better' on the post-test than one whose children began with a score of 100, unless all scores remained the same. Various statistics can be used to try to partial out the effects of initial differences, such as *analysis of covariance* and *regression analysis*. The usual procedure is to take a measure which is thought to affect initial differences, like social class, and use that as part of the procedure in an attempt to 'even up' the groups, but the use of this approach is almost always controversial.

'I've used correlations, analysis of variance, factor analysis and multiple regression, and you still come out stupid'

Figure 5.2 Statistics

Predicting

Regression, particularly *multiple regression analysis,* is often used to make a prediction. One variant of it is *stepwise multiple regression,* which involves taking the predictor which shows the highest correlation with the outcome measure and then combining it step by step with others to improve the correlation. An example would be if the observer wanted to know how best to predict scores on a pupil 'attitude to science' test. There might be a correlation of +0.5 between the attitude scores and a rating measure of teachers' enthusiasm in the classroom. The next best predictor might be a measure of the amount of practical work done, and by combining these two measures, the correlation might go up to +0.7. A third measure, say 'teacher's own knowledge of science', when added to the first two might push the correlation up to +0.8. Stepwise multiple regression rarely produces such neat ordering and high values in real life classroom research, but can still have a place where prediction is of interest.

Reducing complexity

Sometimes researchers find that their data look complex and need reducing in complexity so that sense can be made of what has been found. With large data sets, therefore, *factor analysis* and *cluster analysis* can be used. Factor analysis is a way of putting together sets of measures that correlate with each other and reducing these to fewer factors. Scores gathered by classroom observation using the Flanders FIAC system (described in Chapter 2) might show that short teacher questions, brief pupil answers and praise all correlated quite highly and came together in the same factor. This might be then given a name like 'programmed learning' to reflect the stimulus–response–reinforcement nature of the interactions.

Cluster analysis is another way of putting together scores in more parsimonious form, but this time individual teachers' profiles can be grouped together, in a similar way to creating a taxonomy of plants that are in the same family because they share similar characteristics. There are many forms of cluster analysis that group people's profiles, and Bennett (1976) applied cluster analysis to the questionnaire responses about teaching strategies from a large group of teachers, creating twelve groups whose styles of teaching seemed different from each other.

This brief description of some statistical procedures is by no means complete, and indeed a great deal has been omitted. There are many articles on different aspects of statistics in education in the comprehensive research handbook by Keeves (1988) and novices are urged once more to proceed with caution.

Aggregating findings

There are several ways to put together findings from several different pieces of classroom observation research. The technique of *meta analysis* described and developed by Glass (1978) is a process for aggregating the findings from several studies to see whether they can offer consistent findings. There are two parts to meta analysis, the first being the actual process for putting together data from projects which may have used different statistical procedures, like chi squares, correlations, t tests or F ratios from analysis of variance, and therefore need converting for aggregation. The second part is the devising of an overall effect size, and this can be calculated for all the studies under review, or there can be separate effect sizes for, say, larger and smaller studies (to see whether size of sample makes a difference), older and newer research, or studies judged to be rigorous according to certain criteria, and those deemed to be less so.

Different investigators analysing the same or a similar set of studies can, however, reach different conclusions, depending on what criteria they use for aggregation. Winne (1979) analysed experimental studies of questioning where teachers asked certain types of questions, and came to the conclusion that there was no causal link between asking higher order questions and pupil learning, whereas Redfield and Rousseau (1981), who did a meta analysis of most of the same studies, decided that there was a positive association between higher order cognitive questioning and children's learning.

Small-scale research

Although the best known research projects tend to be the ones that were conducted on a national or international scale and resulted in published books, articles and conference papers, there are numerous small-scale pieces of research that can be important to those who conduct them. Thousands of trainee or experienced teachers and administrators or organisers of projects will undertake an investigation as part of their training or professional work. Thus a trainee teacher might study a teacher at work for a dissertation or term paper, a teacher or head may observe lessons as part of a thesis for an MPhil or PhD. Carefully done, not only is this kind of exercise worthwhile, but also it can fulfil the role which research has done since the beginning of human life, by adding to our stock of knowledge.

Some of the most interesting and significant educational research has been carried out in one school. There are, of course, limitations, but provided that the writer does not make claims that stretch beyond the legitimate confines of the one shot case study, much of value can be learned. *Hightown Grammar* by Lacey (1970) and the account of 'Lumley Secondary Modern' in *Social Relations in a Secondary School* by Hargreaves (1967) were both insightful accounts of individual schools which became significant books in the case study literature.

When Her Majesty's Inspectorate (DES 1978) visited several hundred secondary schools to see how they taught classes of mixed ability, it commented on the comparative reluctance of teachers of mathematics and modern languages to teach classes containing children with a wide variety of achievement. However, this broad brush account lacked the warmth that an in-depth study of real life experience can bring, and it needed the significant case study by Stephen Ball (1981) of 'Beachside Comprehensive' to document more precisely the attitudes and actual classroom practice of teachers in a single school that was changing from a broad banding policy to one of mixed ability classes. This revealed in considerable detail, through accounts of lesson observations and interviews, that it was the mathematics and modern languages staff who were reluctant to make the change, and how the English teachers saw themselves as pioneers.

Individual researchers, especially those working alone on a part-time basis for a degree or wanting to study practice in their own school, face a number of difficulties. Not the least of these is the matter of subjectivity. First time investigators encounter the inevitable criticism that they are not just inexperienced, but likely to view their own school or a single classroom through a distorted lens, having only their own perceptions, experiences and prejudices on which to draw.

A number of procedures can be adopted, however, that will at least minimise this compounded subjectivity, even if they do not eliminate it entirely. It is worth trying to avoid setting up a project in which the investigator is simply seeking to justify his/her practices. Self-evaluation is possible, but only if undertaken with an open mind rather than defensively. This is particularly important for heads or other senior people who carry some responsibility for what goes on in a school, and may be threatened by, rather than relaxed about their own investigation.

Trying to find a second person who may be interested on an occasional basis is also worthwhile, or even someone willing to share the burden of the research more equally, as many teachers have worked as a pair to study their own school or each other's classroom. This is useful for checking one's own interpretation of events, seeing how much agreement there is with another person when using a structured observation schedule, selecting exemplary quotations from interviews or illustrative extracts from lessons, or the double scoring of children's work or the tests they have completed. Most first and higher degree regulations allow for more than one person to collaborate, provided that the final account makes clear who did what. Each of the individual contributions not only must be clearly identifiable, but also must be worthy of the award in its own right.

Valuable work can, therefore, be done on a modest scale of enquiry, and individual investigators should conduct their study as rigorously as possible in the circumstances. They should also try to write and publish an account of what they find in an appropriate journal so that it reaches a wider audience. Among many feasible topics which individuals, pairs or small groups working in modest circumstances can undertake are the following:

1   A study of a single or pair of classrooms over a period of time to document some kind of change, like a new curriculum, a change of teacher, or the effects of a new policy.

2   Observation of all the teachers in the same primary team or secondary subject department, with focus on a particular aspect, such as the teaching of a common theme, like 'electricity' or 'algebra', or on a more general topic such as classroom rules, expectations about pupil work, or the kinds of questions asked.

3   A series of pupil pursuits, as described in Chapter 4, to document the daily experiences of a group of target pupils, preferably avoiding diffusion and concentrating on some predetermined element, such as how they interact with different teachers, what reading and writing they do in a day, how they behave, what they appear to be learning, or how coherent or disordered their day is.

4   A study of one or more groups of children, perhaps those that sit at the same table in a primary school, observing how they interact with each other, the extent to which they collaborate with or hinder one another, the roles played by individual members, how the teacher interacts with them.

5   A modest classroom experiment. One or more teachers can try out two different methods of explaining a new topic, see the effects of summaries given (a) entirely by the pupils, (b) entirely by the teachers, (c) shared by both, or try different approaches to dealing with pupils who misbehave.

Small-scale research can be vitally important to the people who do it, and need not be insignificant to others. Embarking on an enquiry into classroom practice can teach the investigator valuable transferable skills, such as observing and recording, interviewing, data processing and report writing. Though thousands of individual investigators only carry out one enquiry in their lives, and then often for a specific purpose, like obtaining a degree or fulfilling a requirement in a training programme, there are numerous others who, having had the courage to investigate and acquired the relevant skills, do go on to conduct further research on a modest scale. The 'enquiring school' or 'teacher researcher' are concepts worth supporting, and I shall return to them in Chapter 6.

Chapter 6

Observation and action

The dynamic practitioner

The thousands of repeats and rehearsals of favoured teaching styles experienced by teachers over a professional lifetime make for a static rather than dynamic practitioner. It would be easy to acquire a set of strategies that appear to fit cosily, like a favourite pair of slippers, but the rapidly changing world of the late twentieth and early twenty-first centuries requires something much more flexible and imaginative. Alexander *et al.* (1992), in a report on primary teaching commissioned by the Secretary of State, were among many who commended careful scrutiny of classroom processes by the practitioners themselves.

From the very beginning of their career, whether they are in a training institution or a school, new teachers' professional development can be informed by regular and discerning observation of lessons. We found in the Leverhulme Primary Project (Wragg 1993a) that student teachers frequently received little help in the management of their first encounters with pupils at the beginning of their teaching practice. Yet the experienced teachers themselves in the schools we observed had made a massive collective effort to establish sound behaviour management principles in the first week of the school year back in September. By the time students arrived, this collective drive was much more low key.

Many students identify closely with their pupils and sometimes wish to establish a different relationship than the one they inherit. They will need much more help in negotiating this, especially if their early attempts encounter resistance or even hostility. If students do not analyse the situation in which they find themselves, they sometimes, in their attempts to establish a relaxed relationship, find themselves carping and demanding silence all day, filling out the very stereotype they seek to avoid. Yet teachers and supervising tutors sometimes give students a relatively long period in which things may 'settle down', when the early phase of first encounters is often the one that needs most reflection and analysis, even if the 'observation' is indirect, perhaps by verbal report from the student.

The same can be said about the development of experienced teachers' professional skills. The requirement that all teachers should be appraised and that their appraisal should be based, in part at least, on direct observation of their classroom teaching, means that class management, questioning, explaining, subject knowledge, lesson preparation and planning, as well as topics like pupil assessment, should be reviewed as part of a whole school process, not just by each teacher in isolation, a topic to which I shall return below.

In many teacher appraisal schemes, school-based in-service programmes, and even initial teacher training courses, there is still too little attention paid to such important basic classroom skills as questioning and explaining. Yet there have been a number of studies which offer a great deal of information about these skills, even if the evidence does not point unequivocally to the use of any single style. Furthermore, they are skills which can be observed, and which lend themselves especially to discussion and practice in training, whether by beginners or experienced teachers. Students or teachers can note down the written and oral questions asked by teachers they observe or by their fellow students. They can plan and discuss key questions for groups they are teaching, analyse transcripts of lessons to work out the kind of thought or action being elicited by different sorts of questions or by sequences.

There are many experienced teachers who have worked at their professional skills, like questioning, while others have fallen into a routine of asking almost entirely management and data recall questions, which may be unexacting for many of their pupils. Slower learning children are perfectly capable of responding to higher order questions, especially if the teacher sequences them carefully. This was shown in some interesting experimental research and development work at San Francisco State College (Taba 1966; Taba *et al.* 1971). Though she did not always satisfy the research community that her work had been rigorously evaluated, Taba produced teaching modules showing how social studies teachers could ask questions that moved up from simple recall to grouping, labelling, predicting, making inferences and establishing generalisations.

In view of the very large number of questions that many teachers ask, it is important that they reflect on the context and the nature of the topic during which questioning takes place, the demands that questions place on pupils, the appropriateness of the language of questions to the individual or group concerned and the effect of questions on subsequent learning and related activities. It is quite straightforward to set up training programmes, either for beginners or for experienced teachers, to let them explain certain concepts, principles or events to each other or to a group of children, and then analyse an audio or video recording of the explanation. This can be combined with a simple test of recall or interviews with individual pupils to see what they have understood from the explanation. In addition, it is a good safe environment in which people can reflect on the kind of explanation they have given, the extent to which it was helped by diagrams, pictures, questions from the teacher or pupils, examples and illustrations.

Questions and explanations are usually related closely to the nature of the tasks which children undertake in their classroom, whether these are whole class activities or assignments for individuals and small groups, and whether they are given by the teacher, chosen by the pupil or negotiated by both. An interesting and very important observation study by Bennett *et al.* (1984) offered considerable insight into the whole question of the tasks that children are set and the extent to which these match their ability and the current state of their knowledge and skill. They found that less able pupils were often set tasks beyond them and more able pupils were given tasks that were simple for them to complete. It has been a common finding that teachers often tend to teach at or around the middle of the ability range of a class.

The work of Bennett and his colleagues showed how observers can document the work of a particular child so that the teacher can then reflect on the appropriateness of the task to the child concerned. An extract from their account tells the story of twenty-three minutes in the life of a 7 year old:

> Alan was given a writing assignment. His teacher showed him a set of cards, each of which illustrated people at work, and suggested that he write about one of them. He selected a card showing a bus driver and took it to his desk. He paused for 5 minutes, apparently thinking about what to write. Eventually the teacher approached and asked him what his first sentence was going to be. He replied, 'I went on a bus to school'. He started his writing and then searched through his word book for 'school'. He failed to find it and consulted his teacher. She helped him spell it and then explained about the 'sleepy c'. He went back to his desk and continued to write for several minutes, reading aloud as he wrote. He hesitated over the word 'sometimes' and went to the teacher to ask how to spell 'times'. There was a queue at the teacher's desk. Whilst waiting he found the word under 't' in his word book and shouted out to the teacher, 'I've found it miss. It's here'. A few minutes later he went to the teacher again to ask how to spell 'gives' ... Twenty-three minutes after choosing the workcard Alan took his story out to have it marked. He had written, 'I went to school on the bus and I went home on the bus sometimes the bus driver gives me something to eat Im going homs I am going to sleep til morning'.

Such an account might easily have been provided by a fellow teacher, if teachers were working in pairs to study each other's classrooms. The result is not an excuse to snigger about his spelling errors and how Alan had hacked out his story at the rate of slightly over one word a minute; after all, most teachers, if they are busy, will find it difficult to manage every single pupil's work in such a way that the task is exactly right all the time. It is rather an opportunity for both observer and observed to try to improve the process. Did Alan need more structure? Was the topic appropriate? How useful is his word book? What help would he need to be able to use a simple dictionary? How could the teacher generate more independence among the pupils, so that the five minute queues of word seekers diminish or disappear and she is free to help those with real problems, or stimulate to higher and further levels of activity those who finish assignments rapidly? What other forms of class and task management would make the teacher's role more effective?

Trainee teachers can profitably analyse the tasks set by experienced teachers or by fellow students, and this is another activity which can be set up during a training course without a great deal of difficulty. It is also one which has immediate and positive payoff, as novices and experienced teachers can work together to analyse process in a way that all may benefit. The students discover how they might better structure pupils' learning, the teachers put their own or a student's practice under the microscope and modify it for the better in the light of what they learn from the analysis, and not least the pupils may in future, hopefully, be the recipients of more stimulating assignments from teachers, or may themselves develop a bigger stake in what they do if they are party to the consultation process, as they should be.

The question of teacher competencies is often raised by governments (DES 1991) and debate about proficiency raises several important matters, and indeed sometimes arouses strong feelings. Not the least of these is whether teachers should learn their skills in part or as a whole. The extreme part-learning stance is taken by some supporters of competency-based teacher education who believe that the teaching can be atomised into hundreds of discrete mini-acts which can be systematically learned and appraised, and the extreme holist stance is adopted by those who contend that teaching is an art, and to seek to segment it, is to destroy it.

There is considerable interest in the notion of the teacher researcher (Stenhouse 1975) and the reflective practitioner (Schoen 1983). In order to be effective, reflection must be related to action, which it can both precede and follow, and the study and development of classroom skills must not be seen in opposition to other forms of training, but rather as a complement to them. Some emphasis on observing and crafting specific skills in an initial training course, in school-based in-service programme of professional development, in the training of mentors or appraisers, does not replace other forms of reflection and practice, but rather should work in harmony with them. My own inclination has increasingly been to move much more towards an inductive approach to reflection and the teaching of educational theory, starting with classroom observation.

The theory behind the practice should receive much more rigorous scrutiny by teachers who are both reflective and dynamic. Generations of trainee primary teachers in the 1930s, 1940s and even 1950s and beyond were told firmly by many teacher trainers that children should not be taught to read until they were 6. This was based on statements by such as Morphett and Washburne (1931) that children were not ready to read until they had obtained a mental age of 6 years 6 months. It was bunk, and teachers engaged in the sort of inductive experience-led early training I have described above would have reported countless examples to show it was not true. With an inductive approach, bad theory is likely to be seen off. Insightful classroom observation helps sustain both a body of dynamic and discerning teachers, and a school culture can be established which foments the same excitement among teachers about professional self-discovery, as teachers often seek to create with their classes.

The dynamic school

The research literature shows clearly that there is no single good teacher stereo-type, so there is no case for saying that all teachers and students in a school should teach in like manner. Indeed, there are considerable differences, not only in practice, but also in competence, even within the same school. In the Leverhulme Primary Project we found that two teachers in virtually adjacent classrooms in the same school could have vastly different levels of misbehaviour and pupil involvement in the task (Wragg 1993a). Duke (1978) claimed, as a result of his researches, that in schools where behaviour was good, there was clarity among the staff about what was required and what roles and conventions would be adopted. Classroom observation can help teachers understand what is happening in their own classroom and elsewhere, and this is a valuable first step to a collective commitment to working collaboratively to improve teaching in the whole school.

When student teachers come to a school for observation, occasional teaching experience or block practice, they should become part of a school's process of professional self-scrutiny which seems natural and sustained, rather than sculptured and sporadic. There are many ways of establishing such a culture. Tikunoff and Ward (1983) describe how groups of teachers collaborated with higher education institutions to formulate questions and then investigate them. Many teachers following higher degree programmes complete dissertations (as described in Chapter 4) which address directly issues in their school, conducting observation of lessons as part of a rigorous analysis of process.

Most teacher training institutions have numerous tutors who are greatly experienced in the art and craft of lesson observation. They see classes in different schools and acquire considerable expertise in watching and analysing what they see. So too do advisers and advisory teachers who have the opportunity to travel to several schools. This is one of the strengths of a genuine partnership in initial and post-experience training between a teacher training institution and a school. The greater use of lesson analysis through careful observation has been an increasing feature of initial training courses since the 1970s, and it is a pity that courses for experienced teachers have usually put much less weight on observation.

Wright (1992) gives an account of how several teachers implemented a reading recovery programme aimed at helping children with reading problems. Although there is often dispute about the long-term effectiveness of such intervention programmes, experiments of this kind really involve teachers in self-observation, as well as observation of pupils' behaviour and learning. Not every instance of classroom observation has to involve outsiders, and the act of trying to detect what children can and cannot do, taking action, and evaluating the outcome, involves careful observation of oneself. In the dynamic school a variety of such programmes over a number of years would be commonplace. These would not be so frequent as to disorientate people or create anxiety, but often enough for worthwhile improvements to take place.

There are many tools available for helping schools scrutinise their own practice. In the Teacher Education Project, in which hundreds of secondary school lessons were studied from 1976 to 1981, and the Leverhulme Primary Project, which pursued similar strategies in primary schools from 1988 to 1992, several workbooks were produced on topics like class management (Wragg 1981, 1993b), group work (Kerry and Sands 1982; Dunne and Bennett 1990), questioning (Kerry 1982; Brown and Wragg 1993), explaining (Brown and Hatton 1982; Wragg and Brown 1993) and other topics, with practical activities which allow either trainee or experienced teachers, or both, first to reflect on practice and then to try and improve it.

There are other projects and publications which invite teachers to scrutinise their own practice in a particular way; many new curricula for science and technology, mathematics, modern languages, humanities subjects, physical and health education, or creative arts, make assumptions that teachers will do precisely this, whether they are primary or secondary, teach single subjects, operate through topic and project work, or mix their approaches. Questioning the most effective use of whole class teaching, group and individual work, honing the management of one's lessons, considering the relevant subject matter and how children can best learn it, lie at the very heart of self-analysis, for novice or expert.

Nor need such scrutiny be confined to teachers. If pupils are thought to be knowledgeable and insightful about teaching, then perhaps there should be much more discussion with them about teaching and learning. Schmuck and Schmuck (1975) describe how the teacher can sensitise children working in groups to the processes involved, and capitalise on their natural insights to make them partners in learning, rather than merely the recipients of teaching. When classes are badly behaved it should be possible for pupils and teachers to analyse together why relationships are poor.

Sadly, those teachers with ineffective class management are the very ones who are least likely to be able to do this, and it may need another person to join them, an external tutor, trusted colleague or deputy head, with all the threat that that offers to the teacher's sense of personal and professional competence. Experiments involving children in talking about what have often been teachers' professional secrets may be preferable to the traditional tendency to leave students or experienced teachers who are having discipline problems to flounder on with little support. The sensible use of 'circle time', when pupils and teacher sit and talk about behaviour problems, ground rules, learning difficulties, or whatever else is legitimately on such an agenda, can enhance learning, but not if self-confrontation is seen as a threat or becomes overdone and self-indulgent.

In a dynamic school the dividing line between initial training and in-service professional development becomes almost non-existent, as the interests and aspirations of the two groups coalesce. If student teachers did not exist, then one very effective way of stimulating experienced teachers to improve their own classroom practice would be to invent them. Yet it is still the case that relatively few teachers have been trained properly to analyse their own teaching in a systematic way, or to study the practice of others. It is regrettable that teaching has so fully absorbed the time and energy of practitioners themselves that they have rarely, in some cases never, had the opportunity to watch and reflect on the practices of others at work.

That is why it may be advisable for a school wishing to tool itself up for more effective self-scrutiny to draw up a three year development plan, which would allow teachers to become better trained to observe lessons, the visiting of classrooms in other schools, identifying a manageable set of projects that would involve some self-scrutiny among pairs of teachers, or by those who work in the same subject department, and the devising of an outline of professional progression that had some agreement among staff. In class management, for example, a notion like 'organise the handing-out and collection of materials' might be a fairly basic matter, involving a teacher thinking about how this can best be organised. Indeed children themselves could work it out. On the other hand, 'judging the right language register, appropriate response to and suitable activities for a pupil bewildered by a new mathematical or scientific concept' clearly exerts much higher level of intellectual and practical demand.

With all these blue skies ideals, of course, there is a price to pay. Someone must eventually sit down and translate them into action, and it is at this point that one runs into the realities of shortage of time, money, resources and sheer nervous energy. Most people could quite legitimately say that they were too busy to visit someone else's classroom, that the school was so strapped that no one could be spared even for a second, or that everyone felt defensive enough nowadays, without adding to the strain through being observed and possibly filleted by someone observing lessons. Yet if teaching is to develop to the point where it can display its talents with pride and its frailties without fear, a tall order in a climate where teachers have often been criticised unfairly and blamed for society's ills, then positive steps must be taken, however busy people are, to make lesson observation a high priority, and that may mean ingenuity, and capitalising on what is available, like the presence of student teachers and their tutors.

Ten working examples of classroom observation in action

In order to give more direct insight into how observation and action can be linked, especially to help experienced and beginner teachers develop further their own professional skills, and also encourage pupils to learn more effectively, here are ten examples of classroom observation being used to target certain aspects of teaching and learning. They cover a variety of age groups and topics, and the areas of focus include trying to improve pupil learning and behaviour, as well as honing such professional skills as class discipline, time management, questioning and explaining. All should be possible, given goodwill and ingenuity, of being accommodated into normal school practice and staff development procedures, though some rethinking of how teachers are deployed may be necessary.

In essence they are all mini 'action research' projects, based on real events, involving teachers first in studying the processes in their own classroom, then taking some action which will hopefully be for the better, before monitoring the outcome. Doing research on one's own practice may be problematic, for the reasons given in earlier chapters, but it can also be exciting and a good example for children. Teachers who are curious, enquiring and innovating offer a role model to children they are encouraging to do the same. If they are dull, safe, unquestioning and stuck in a rut, they can hardly expect their pupils to be the exact opposite.

Learning opportunities for 3–4 year olds

Question

A group of teachers in a nursery school are concerned that boys appear to be happiest engaging in noisy play, while girls show little interest in a number of the activities available. *Are their assumptions justified? What is actually happening during the day, and should they do anything about it?*

Observation

The head and staff decide what aspects they want to focus on, and an 'early years' student teacher is asked (a) to watch four children, two boys and two girls, for five minutes each, twenty minutes in all; (b) to make notes on what each child is doing and talk to them to get their own explanations of what is going on.

During each five minute observation period of a particular child, the student makes notes under four headings:

1   interaction with others
2   language behaviour
3   nature of task/activity
4   pupil involvement in task/activity.

Subsequently each child is asked: 'Can you tell me a bit about what you've just been doing …'. Spontaneous prompts are used as appropriate, such as: 'What were you and Robert talking about?' or 'What did you think of the story about the jumping bean?' The student also talks to the teacher concerned about events.

After five such twenty minute observations of four different children each time, the student then presents an oral report to the staff for discussion. It turns out that the boys rarely talk to each other during the more boisterous activities, because they seem to prefer charging round the room uttering racing car noises and sound effects. Some teachers discourage this because they believe it is dangerous, while others refer to it as 'fantasy play' and ask children to tell them about it. A number of girls say they don't like making things as they prefer playing at dressing up, or hearing a story.

The staff discuss the findings and compare similarities and differences in their practice. They decide to engage the boys more in conversation about their rough and tumble fantasy play and to encourage them to talk to the others publicly about the games they like. They talk to the girls about what they like and dislike about the various 'making' activities on offer and widen the scope of what they cover. The student teacher is invited later in the term to make further observations to see if there are any changes.

Self-confidence in the reception class

Question

A few children in the reception class appear to be less involved and more withdrawn during lessons. Some appear lost or uncertain about what they are doing, or take a long time over a task that others complete quickly. *Why are some children really on the fringe of the newcomers, and can anything be done to bring them more into the centre?*

Observation

A classroom assistant is asked to look out for certain children who appear to be among those causing concern. Each day she keeps a distant eye on one particular child, taking any natural opportunities that arise to go over and monitor what that child is doing, engaging him or her in conversation.

Observation shows that the children are not usually being disruptive in any way. They tend to be anxious and want to see what others are doing before starting their own work. Some seek out one other pupil to shadow and become overly dependent, unable or unwilling to act on their own. They rarely initiate and tend not to volunteer to speak during class discussions, talking only when called on by the teacher.

The teacher initiates a procedure whereby two children are 'special' each day, allowed to give out and collect things, assist the teacher, be first to choose, etc. They are also encouraged to answer questions from a small group or from the whole class on matters such as: what pet they would like; what their favourite birthday present would be; what they enjoy most on television and why; what they like best in school. Eventually every pupil will have been 'special', but the classroom assistant observes any of the 'withdrawn' children to see if being special seems to make any difference to their behaviour and feelings. She talks regularly to them as well in a natural and unforced way, without making them too self-conscious.

Time for individual work with 7 year olds

Question

A teacher feels that he has little time for individual work with his class of 7 year old children, often being buried under a long queue of pupils waiting to see him, or sitting with their hand in the air when they are supposed to be working at their assignment. *Why does the teacher become marooned at his desk, and how can he create more quality time to spend with individuals and small groups?*

Observation

The teacher shares his concern with others and finds that they too would like to find more time for individual monitoring. The school arranges for two classes to be combined for story assembly, or other larger group activity, so that one teacher can be released for half an hour. This means that the Year 2 teacher can be observed by a colleague and can also observe another teacher at work.

The observer talks to any child entering the queue to see the teacher, or sitting with hand in the air trying to attract the teacher's attention, saying: 'Can I help?' and then noting down the nature of the query or problem. Analysis of these show that the three most common reasons why many children seek the teacher's attentions are

1   they want to know how to spell a word
2   they have reached a certain point in their task and are looking for approval to carry on
3   they are complaining about another pupil disrupting their work.

The general problem, with individual variations, seems to be one of too much dependency on the teacher.

The teacher tries to create greater independence. He discusses the problem with the class, pointing out that he cannot spend all the time he would like with them, because he gets so many interruptions. He addresses specifically the points that have come up from his colleague's observations, asking questions like, 'What can you do if you can't spell a word?' He also devotes more time to practising alphabetical order and showing children how to find words in a dictionary, so they can check their own spellings. He discovers, from observing some of his colleagues, how they generate greater independence, so occasionally he issues messages like, 'Back your own judgement', 'See if you can decide for yourself', 'Discuss it with someone else on your table', 'Only ask me if you're really stuck' or 'For the next ten minutes I want to work with certain children, so please get on with your work and don't interrupt me unless the school is on fire'.

During later observations, his colleagues try to see if members of his class have, in practice, become independent and if he does manage to find more time for better quality interactions and conversations with individuals and small groups.

The behaviour of junior school pupils

Question

By common agreement among teachers in a junior school, the pupils aged 8 and 9 seem less well behaved than other classes, whether this is in the playground or in lessons. *Are their suppositions about pupils' misbehaviour true and, if so, what can they do to improve matters?*

Observation

Some baseline information needs to be gathered first. The school has two student teachers on teaching practice. The staff and the university tutor responsible for the students work out a schedule with the students of how the observation can be done. The students will be able to use the data for their college-based assignment, as part of their training course, so they read some of the classroom management literature.

Using a modification of the Exeter schedule (described in Chapter 2), they look for examples of misbehaviour and the response to it in different classrooms. They also observe in the playground to see who is misbehaving there, and note the name and age group of the children concerned. They find that there is indeed a greater incidence of disruptive and anti-social behaviour in the middle years of the junior school.

The three most common manifestations of it in the classroom are

1   noisy chatter, with the teacher often telling children to be quiet, which works for a while until the noise escalates again
2   illicit movement, when children get out of their seat without permission, often going over to another table and distracting children there from their work
3   challenges to the teacher's authority, with some pupils regularly questioning why they should have to do what is being asked of them.

In the playground the most frequent disturbances are caused when the game of one group interferes with the game of another, for example, when a game of football strays into the territory of a group playing at chasing each other.

Teachers interview some of the more disruptive children and discover that the class work is not sufficiently differentiated. The more able find it banal, the less able are confused. They review the tasks being set for 8 and 9 year olds to try to match them more closely to individuals where possible. They also encourage the pupils themselves to take more responsibility for their own behaviour and progress, initiating a 'self-evaluation' scheme, which requires the children, every so often, to comment on and monitor their own progress, both in their academic work and behaviour. Teachers and pupils discuss the meaning, as well as the implications in practice, of words and phrases like 'co-operation' or 'respect for one another'. Pupils use a 'certainly true', 'sometimes true' and 'not true' rating of themselves, for categories such as 'I usually get on with my work', 'I check through what I have done' and 'I distract other children'.

In the playground the teachers change supervision duty arrangements, so that more time is spent anticipating trouble, rather than letting it happen and then merely responding to it. Potential flashpoints, such as the border area between children who are playing two different games, are monitored and patrolled more frequently. Teachers move towards any suggestion of physical aggression or intimidation before it has escalated and discuss what is happening with those concerned. There is a later monitoring by the two student teachers using the same procedures as before, to see what, if anything, has changed, and they then discuss with the teachers whether any changes are for the better.

The achievement of 10 year old boys

Question

Each year the reading and language test results of 10 year old boys in two parallel classes are significantly lower than those of the girls in the same two groups. *Is there anything happening in the classroom that might contribute to this lower level of achievement, and can teachers take any steps to improve what they do for boys, without prejudicing the education of the girls in the class?*

Observation

This is a commonly observed phenomenon. At the age of 11 there can be 10 per cent fewer boys obtaining an 'average' or 'above average' grade in reading and language tests, and by the age of 16 this can have grown to a 20 per cent gap between them in a GCSE English examination. The explanations may be complex, not only to do with the functioning of the brain, but also reflecting the attitudes and values of a wider society. If they are indeed neurological or socially constructed, they may, to some extent, lie outside the control of teachers. Nonetheless, there may be a classroom element worth pursuing.

The two teachers decide to ask for supply teacher cover, as part of their own professional development programme, so that they can observe each other's lessons, when 'English' is on the timetable. They undertake a mixture of observation and interviewing. By interviewing each other's classes they discover that most boys feel that the books they are asked to read in school are tedious. Many boys say they prefer books on sport, adventure and humour, whereas girls often express a preference for fiction over non-fiction.

They work out an agreed observation schedule in two parts. The first part codes teachers' interactions with boys and girls separately, trying to elicit if they are in any way different. The second involves looking for critical events: any single happening which might have a differential effect on boys or girls. They then discuss their findings. It transpires that both teachers often reprimand boys, sometimes for making derogatory comments when pupils say they like a particular book. Girls are more frequently praised for the content and quality of their writing. When children are asked to read silently, the girls are usually more engaged in the task than the boys.

Both teachers resolve to review not only their styles of teaching, but also the types of books they offer to different pupils, opting for a mixture of pupil choice and teacher direction. They each discuss with their own class the differences in test scores obtained by boys and girls in previous years and ask if there are any explanations or suggestions. They arrange for pupils to monitor their own progress more carefully, and decide to appraise the situation again at some future date by arranging more reciprocated observation later in the year.

The transition from primary to secondary school

Question

Pupils transfer from a cluster of small or medium sized junior schools to a large secondary school. There are general and specific questions about the transfer process. The general question is, *in classroom terms, whether the transition from primary to secondary education is a smooth one.* There is also a specific question: *there is a suggestion that pupils' proficiency in certain aspects of mathematics seems to decline during the early part of secondary education, so (a) is this true, and (b) if it is, why might it be happening and what could be done to address the problem?*

Observation

Teachers who teach in the lower years of the secondary school meet together with those who teach in the upper years of a feeder primary school. They decide to visit each other's school to observe lessons. The observation record is in two parts

1   making notes about general similarities and differences in classroom rules, expectations about written work and homework
2   specific focus on the teaching of mathematics, with emphasis on content, styles of teaching and assessment.

They draw up a semi-structured observation sheet for each, consisting of a series of subheadings with space below for comments.

The teachers meet to discuss what they have each seen. Under the heading 'classroom rules' they discover that there is great freedom of movement in the primary school – children may walk across the room, approach the teacher, even leave the classroom, with permission, to go to the library and resource centre – but secondary pupils have to ask permission to get out of their seat. It is also apparent that, in the secondary school, many subject teachers set a single piece of required homework at the end of individual lessons, whereas in the primary school there is less homework, and the class teacher offers more choices.

In mathematics they discover that secondary teachers, believing certain topics may not have been covered thoroughly in the primary school, revisit them in the first year of secondary. They also find that in the secondary school there is a much clearer division in teaching various sub-topics, such as 'number' or 'shape and space', compared with the primary school. Tests of mathematical competence are

Figure 6.1 Top primary pupils – how will secondary school be different?

given, and these reveal that pupils have indeed declined in the field of 'number', but have made considerable progress in 'data handling'. Interviews with lower secondary pupils suggest that maths is seen as more boring in the secondary school than in primary, and that many pupils complain about activities they have already done, at as young an age as 9, being repeated again.

Primary teachers alert their pupils to some of the differences they will experience in the secondary school, especially in classroom rules and homework conventions. The visiting days, when children make a preliminary visit to their new secondary school in July, are redesigned with several actual lessons inserted, instead of a conducted tour and discussion. A decision is made to review maths teaching in both the primary and secondary school.

Inspectors criticise a foreign language department

Question

A school inspection produces the comment that the pronunciation and intonation of children learning French is generally poor, and that the problem starts at the very beginning with the youngest age group of beginners. *Do children in the first year of secondary school really speak with a poor accent and intonation, and if so, what can be done to improve the foundations being laid for later learning?*

Observation

The members of the modern language department decide to observe each other teaching, particularly in the early years of secondary school. Their focus is on pupils' mispronunciation in particular. They write down verbatim, with a comment, any word or phrase which seems to have been more than usually misspoken, under subheadings such as 'word mispronounced' and 'poor intonation'. They also note down 'teacher's action', if anything appears noteworthy.

Several findings emerge. One is that many pupils appear to have difficulty with the French 'u' and 'r' sound, a word like 'tu' often being spoken as 'chew'. Another is that the wrong syllable of a word, or even the wrong word, is often stressed. They also notice that certain individual children never speak a single word of French during an entire lesson, even when there have been extensive oral exchanges. During group repetition, when the whole class, or a group of pupils chant a response, the pace is often slow and the poorest speakers appear to drag down the quality of what is chanted, making it sound dull and dreary, with little resemblance to a native speaker's intonation.

A further interesting finding is that some teachers say that, because a colleague is scrutinising their teaching and they know what the focus of attention is, they are actually correcting more frequently and offering more pupils a further chance to improve their first effort. They decide to be more rigorous over pronunciation and intonation in the early stages, without becoming so pedantic that children are put off, or made to feel a failure. They map out the survival vocabulary that will be needed to sustain more of the lesson in French, teaching children the appropriate phrases for 'listen carefully', 'say it again', 'well done' and so on.

Explaining complex science concepts to secondary pupils

Question

Teachers in a secondary school science department discover that pupils in the middle years appear not to understand certain key concepts in science. A number of them say they would like to study science at a higher level, but they are worried whether they will cope, as they are already struggling to cope. *Which topics cause pupils greatest difficulty, and how can teachers explain them more clearly?*

Observation

Members of the school science department decide to interview a selection of pupils of different ability to check their understanding of some of the key concepts in science. They identify several, mainly in physical science, which pupils find confusing, or claim not to grasp at all, topics like 'isotopes' and 'forces and acceleration'. Each teacher agrees to explain one of these key concepts while being observed by a colleague. The observer records the main features of the explanation, the strategies used, noting any visual or other aids, writing down verbatim any questions asked by teacher or pupil and the response. After the 'explaining' lesson a selection of children is again interviewed to see what has been understood, what misconceptions there are, and what pupils liked or disliked about the explanation.

Discussion and analysis shows a wide range of strategies being employed. Some teachers explain entirely by question and answer: 'Does the word "isotope" mean anything to you?'; 'Can anyone give me an example?'. Others give their own explanation, without any pupil interaction. Some use analogies: 'It's like ...', while others tell stories about the application of the scientific principle in the everyday world. One teacher uses a video from the school resource centre that other teachers did not realise existed.

Interviews with pupils reveal that they remember most vividly answers to certain questions and concrete examples. Many comment favourably on the teacher who told them how carbon dating worked, and that this helped them understand isotopes better. The opportunity to ask questions during the explanation is particularly valued, especially from the pupils whose teacher split the explanation into smaller sections and checked understanding at each stage. Some children complain that key aspects of the explanation had not been mentioned at all, so there had been no *opportunity to learn*. These comments and the observation findings are discussed by the teachers and several say they will modify their teaching in future in the light of this structured feedback.

Physical education lessons with adolescents

Question

Teachers in a secondary school physical education (PE) department are disappointed that many of the boys appear to have lost interest in any kind of physical activity other than football, and that most girls say they 'hate' PE, regularly bringing sick notes to allow them to be excused. *Why is the current PE programme so unappealing, what are pupils asked to do in lessons, and can a more effective programme be devised?*

Observation

A student teacher is asked to observe several PE lessons, using an observation schedule which notes the type of activity undertaken. He also studies five individual pupils, chosen at random, and video records each of them for a three minute observation period. The pupils are then shown the video and interviewed to elicit their reactions.

Analysis of observations, videos and interviews shows that some children do virtually nothing during certain activities. There seems to be a great deal of waiting one's turn. One pupil is shown merely watching others for the whole of the three minute period, while the teacher is at the other end of the gym working with a different group. Interviews with pupils reveal that many find activities like gymnastics tedious and uninspiring. They cannot, they say, see the purpose of it. Girls in particular say that PE is sweaty and unfeminine, bad for their image, and they hate the clothes they have to wear.

Teachers devise some new elements, involving pupils in the design of them. Girls enjoy aerobics, especially as it is being linked to 'health and beauty', including a study of diet and the purpose of exercise. They particularly like being able to wear leotards instead of gym kit, and choosing some of the music played during aerobics sessions. Further videos show that the girls now engage in vastly more energetic movement during PE than they did previously and the sick notes decline remarkably. Boys enjoy working in groups and setting themselves targets, recording their own progress over a period of time. Although they much prefer playing actual games, they say they can see, from their own recordings and the videos, that their own proficiency in certain sports is improving as a result of the small group skill practices. Teachers find particularly helpful the student teacher being able to video individuals and groups they are not able to watch in detail themselves while they are actually teaching.

Pupils' ability to answer public examination questions

Question

The head of a secondary school is concerned that a group of A level pupils in history is doing less well than in their other chosen subjects. Parents have complained that students frequently obtain one or even two grades lower in history and this spoils their children's portfolio of grades for university entrance. *Why do they do less well, and can better classroom practice be devised to help improve examination performance?*

Observation

The head brings in an external consultant, known to and respected by the history teachers, who observes a number of lessons, having agreed an observation structure with them in advance. Sample timed history questions are answered by pupils under normal public examination conditions. These are read and graded by the external consultant, who also discusses the written answers with both pupils and teachers.

Classroom observations focus on the teaching strategies being used, the role played by pupils in lessons and any relationship there appears to be between what pupils write under examination conditions and what happens in class. Some issues become clear, others remain diffuse. A great deal of transmission of factual material takes place during the observations, when teachers give information which pupils are expected to write down or remember. Sometimes printed handouts are distributed, but then not discussed. Interviews reveal that pupils say they cannot see the links between what they hear in class and the more penetrating questions they are asked in exams. They are expected to be able to engage in critical analysis of historical events, yet much of the classroom interaction observed is descriptive, rather than analytical.

An example noted by the observer occurs when a pupil who asks, 'Why did Austria do so well out the Congress of Vienna?', is given the somewhat vague answer, 'There were several reasons, it's very complicated'. The consultant reaches the painful conclusion that some teachers' own subject knowledge is not secure or comprehensive. They appear to be playing safe by predominantly giving information, discouraging discussion, keeping control over the knowledge purveyed, avoiding the exposure of their own ignorance on certain topics. This appears to frustrate especially the more able and enthusiastic pupils, who have to find out for themselves not only the relevant wider factual information, but teach themselves how to apply and relate it to other knowledge.

The consultant recommends that certain teachers should update and extend their own historical knowledge, be bolder in their teaching and use a wider variety of strategies, encourage pupils to explore the subject for themselves, be prepared to analyse more critically in lessons the topics being taught, and to address specifically the question of examination technique for a subject like history. This is an interesting example of the use of an external consultant who has little of the baggage and tribal loyalty of the internal lesson observer, has higher status than a student or classroom assistant, and may not be afraid to be critical of the teaching observed, but who must, nonetheless, win the confidence and respect of those observed.

Endnote

These ten examples all seem to run wonderfully well, as they can in a book. I have simplified actual events into 'ideal types', to make the individual model read more clearly. Real classroom life is, of course, much more craggy and problematic: one teacher does not want to join in, someone is away ill at the critical moment, pupils in interview say, 'Dunno' or 'It's just boring', there is no available student teacher to do some observation, the school has no money to pay for supply cover while teachers observe each other or visit another school. Yet it is possible to observe oneself and others and improve practice. Many teachers will teach for thirty years or more. It must surely be feasible, on a few occasions at least, to observe and be observed, purely for professional improvement, even in adverse conditions.

I shall finish by describing a model that is well worth imitating, though it occurred in the most unpromising and unlikely circumstances. A few years ago I visited a friend in the United States who was principal of a large high school in Brooklyn, in one of the toughest parts of New York. There were 7,000 pupils and on each of the days I visited some 1,200 were absent from school; over 600 pupils did not speak English. On the first day of the school year some 600 pupils had turned up unexpectedly. There was gang violence, a serious drugs problem, and pupils had been raped and murdered on their way to or from school. Yet every day he could manage it, this principal, who could be forgiven for pleading pressing previous engagements, would watch at least one lesson and discuss it with the teacher. Amid all the mayhem, he believed that trying to improve the quality of teaching by joining his colleagues to look at and share the action, was one of the most valuable things he could do, and he was probably right.

References

Adams, R. S. and Biddle, B. J. (1970) *Realities of Teaching*, New York: Holt, Rinehart & Winston.

Alexander, R., Rose, J. and Woodhead, C. (1992) *Curriculum Organisation and Classroom Practice in Primary Schools: a Discussion Paper*, London: Department of Education and Science.

Allen, D. and Ryan, K. (1969) *Micro-teaching*, Reading, Mass: Addison-Wesley.

Bales, R. F. (1950) *Interaction Process Analysis: a Method for the Study of Small Groups*, Reading, Mass: Addison-Wesley.

Ball, S. (1981) *Beachside Comprehensive: a Case Study of Secondary Schooling*, Cambridge: Cambridge University Press.

Barnes, D., Britton, J. and Rosen, H. (1967) *Language, the Learner and the School*, Harmondsworth: Penguin.

Bennett, N. (1976) *Teaching Styles and Pupil Progress*, London: Open Books.

Bennett, N., Desforges, C., Cockburn, A. and Wilkinson, B. (1984) *The Quality of Pupil Learning Experiences*, London: Lawrence Erlbaum.

Berliner, D. and Tikunoff, W. (1976) 'The California beginning teacher evaluation study: overview of the ethnographic study', *Journal of Teacher Education* **xxviii** (1).

Biddle, B. J. (1989) 'Implications of government funding policies for research on teaching and teacher education: United States of America', *Teaching and Teacher Education* 5 (4): 275–81.

Bloom, B. S. (1956) *Taxonomy of Educational Objectives*, New York: Longmans, Green.

Bridges, E. M. (1986) *The Incompetent Teacher*, Lewes: Falmer Press.

Brophy, J. (1981) 'Teacher praise: a functional analysis', *Review of Educational Research* **51**: 5–32.

Brown, G. A. and Hatton, N. (1982) *Explanations and Explaining*, London: Macmillan.

Brown, G. A. and Wragg, E. C. (1993) *Questioning*, London: Routledge.

Bryman, A. (1988) *Quantity and Quality in Social Research*, London: Unwin Hyman.

Butler, S. ([1872] 1996) *Erewhon*, Ware: Wordsworth Classics.

Campbell, D. T. and Stanley, J. C. (1963) 'Experimental and quasi-experimental designs for research' in N. L. Gage (ed.) *Handbook of Research on Teaching*, Chicago: Rand McNally.

Cohen, L. (1976) *Educational Research in Classrooms and Schools*, London: Harper & Row.

Delamont, S. (1976) *Interaction in the Classroom*, London: Methuen.

Denzin, N. K. (1985) 'Triangulation', in T. Husen and T. N. Postlethwaite (eds) *International Encyclopedia of Educational Research* **9:** 5293–95, Oxford: Pergamon.

DES (1978) *Mixed Ability Work in Comprehensive Schools*, London: HMSO.

DES (1991) *HMI Survey of Competencies in Teacher Education*, London: DES.

Deutsch, M. (1960) 'Minority group and class status as related to social and personality factors in scholastic achievement', *Society for Applied Anthropology Monograph no. 2*, Ithaca, NY: Society for Applied Anthropology.

Dewey, J. (1916) *Democracy and Education*, New York: Macmillan.

Duke, D. L. (1978) 'How the adults in your schools can cause student discipline and what to do about it', *American School Board Journal* **165** (6): 29–30.

Dunne, E. and Bennett, N. (1990) *Talking and Learning in Groups*, London: Macmillan.

Edwards, A. D. and Westgate, D. P. G. (1987) *Investigating Classroom Talk*, Lewes: Falmer Press.

Eggleston, J. F., Galton, M. J. and Jones, M. (1975) *Final Report of the Schools Council Project for the Evaluation of Science Teaching*, London: Macmillan.

Flanagan, J. C. (1949) 'Critical requirements: a new approach to employee evaluation', *Personnel Psychology* **2:** 419–25.

Flanders, N. A. (1970) *Analyzing Teaching Behavior*, Reading, Mass: Addison-Wesley.

Gage, N. L. (1978) *The Scientific Basis of the Art of Teaching*, New York: Teachers College Press.

Gage, N. L. (1985) *Hard Gains in the Soft Sciences*, Bloomington, Ind: Phi Delta Kappa.

Glass, G. V. (1978) 'Integrating findings: the meta-analysis of research', in L. S. Schulman (ed.) *Review of Research in Education*, vol. 5, Itasca, Ill: F. E. Peacock.

Guilford, J. P. (1954) *Psychometric Methods*, New York: McGraw-Hill.

Hall, E. T. (1963) 'A system for the notation of proxemic behavior', *American Anthropologist* **65**. 1003–26.

Hargreaves, D. H. (1967) *Social Relations in a Secondary School*, London: Routledge.

Harvard, G. and Dunne, E. (1992) 'The role of the mentor in developing teacher competence', *Westminster Studies in Education* vol. 15, Oxford: Carfax.

Herbert, J. (1967) *A System for Analysing Lessons*, New York: Teachers College Press.

Jackson, P. W. (1962) 'The way teaching is', *NEA Journal* [National Education Association] **54**: 10–13.

Jackson, P. W. (1968) *Life in Classrooms*, New York: Holt, Rinehart & Winston.

Keeves, J. P. (ed.) (1988) *Educational Research, Methodology and Measurement: An International Handbook*, Oxford: Pergamon.

Kelly, G. A. (1955) *The Psychology of Personal Constructs*, vols 1 and 2, New York: Norton.

Kerlinger, F. N. (1973) *Foundations of Behavioural Research*, 2nd edn, London: Holt, Rinehart & Winston.

Kerry, T. (1982) *Effective Questioning*, London: Macmillan.

Kerry, T. and Sands, M. K. (1982) *Handling Classroom Groups*, London: Macmillan.

King, R. A (1978) *All Things Bright and Beautiful?*, Chichester: Wiley.

King, R. A. (1984) 'The man in the Wendy House', in R. G. Burgess (ed.) *The Research Process in Educational Settings: Ten Case Studies*, Lewes: Falmer Press.

Lacey, C. (1970) *Hightown Grammar*, Manchester: Manchester University Press.

Lorenz, K. (1966) *On Aggression*, New York: Harcourt, Brace and World.

McIntyre, D. (1977) 'Microteaching practice, collaboration with peers and supervisory feedback as determinants of the effects of microteaching', in D. McIntyre, G. MacLeod and R. Griffiths (eds) *Investigations of Microteaching*, London: Croom Helm.

Malinowski, B. (1922) *Argonauts of the Western Pacific: An Account of Native Enterprise and Adventure in the Archipelagoes of Melanesian New Guinea*, London: Routledge.

Mead, G. H. (1934) *Mind, Self and Society*, Chicago: University of Chicago Free Press.

Morphett, M. V. and Washburne, C. (1931) 'When should children begin to read?' *Elementary School Journal* **31**: 496–503.

Nash, R. (1973) *Classrooms Observed*, London: Routledge.

Oppenheim, A. N. (1992) *Questionnaire Design: Interviewing and Attitude Measurement*, London: Pinter.

Piaget, J. (1954) *The Construction of Reality in the Child*, New York: Basic Books.

Powney, J. and Watts, M. (1987) *Interviewing in Educational Research*, London: Routledge.

Redfield, D. L. and Rousseau, E. W. (1981) 'A meta-analysis of experimental research on teacher questioning behaviour', *Review of Educational Research* **51**: 237–45.

Rogers, C. R. (1970) *On Being a Person*, Boston, Mass: Houghton-Mifflin.

Rosenshine, B. and Furst, N. (1973) 'The use of direct observation to study teaching', in R. W. Travers (ed.) *Second Handbook of Research on Teaching*, Chicago: Rand McNally.

Rowe, M. B. (1972) 'Wait-time and rewards as instructional variables', paper presented at the National Association for Research in Science Teaching, Chicago, April.

Ryans, D. G. (1960) *Characteristics of Teachers*, Washington, DC: American Council on Education.

Samph, T. (1976) 'Observer effects on teacher verbal behaviour', *Journal of Educational Psychology* **68** (6): 736–41.

Schmuck, R. A and Schmuck, P. A. (1975) *Group Processes in the Classroom*, Dubuque, Iowa: William C. Brown.

Schoen, D. (1983) *The Reflective Practitioner*, New York: Basic Books

Schutz, A. (1972) *The Phenomenology of the Social World*, London: Heinemann.

Sharp, R. and Green, A. (1975) *Education and Social Control*, London: Routledge & Kegan Paul.

Sinclair, J. and Coulthard, M. (1975) *Towards an Analysis of Discourse: the Language of Teachers and Pupils*, London: Oxford University Press.

Skinner, B. F. (1954) 'The science of learning and the art of teaching', *Harvard Educational Review* **24**: 86–97.

Stenhouse, L. (1975) *An Introduction to Curriculum Research and Development*, London: Heinemann.

Stevens, R. (1912) 'The question as a measure of efficiency in teaching', *Teachers College Contributions to Education*, 48, Columbia University, New York.

Stones, E. (1984) *Supervision in Teacher Education: a Counselling and Pedagogical Approach*, London: Methuen.

Stubbs, M. (1983) *Language, Schools and Classrooms*, 2nd edn, London: Methuen.

Taba, H. (1966) *Teaching Strategies and Cognitive Functioning in Elementary School Children,* USOE Cooperative Research Project 1574, San Francisco, Calif: San Francisco State College.

Taba, H., Durkin, M. C., Fraenkel, J. R. and McNaughton, A H. (1971) *A Teacher's Handbook to Elementary Social Studies*, 2nd edn, Reading, Mass: Addison-Wesley.

Tikunoff, W. J. and Ward, B. A. (1983) 'Collaborative research on teaching', *Elementary School Journal* **83** (1): 453–68.

Tizard, B. and Hughes, M. (1984) *Young Children Learning: Talking and Thinking at Home and at School*, London: Fontana.

Weber, M. (1947) *The Theory of Social and Economic Organization*, New York: Free Press.

Winne, P. H. (1979) 'Experiments relating teachers' use of higher cognitive questions to student achievement', *Review of Educational Research* **49**: 13–50.

Withall, J. (1949) 'The development of a technique for the measurement of social-emotional climate in the classroom', *Journal of Experimental Education* **17**: 347–61.

Wragg, E. C. (1973) 'A study of student teachers in the classroom', in G. Chanan, (ed.) *Towards a Science of Teaching*, Slough: National Foundation for Educational Research.

Wragg, E. C. (1974) *Teaching Teaching*, Newton Abbot: David & Charles.

Wragg, E. C. (1981) *Class Management and Control*, London: Macmillan.

Wragg, E. C. (1982) *Review of Research in Teacher Education*, Windsor: NFER-Nelson.

Wragg, E. C. (ed.) (1984) *Classroom Teaching Skills*, London: Croom Helm.

Wragg, E. C. (1993a) *Primary Classroom Skills*, London: Routledge.

Wragg, E. C. (1993b) *Class Management*, London: Routledge.

Wragg, E. C. (1997) 'To hell and back', *Times Educational Supplement* 21 November.

Wragg, E. C. and Brown, G. A. (1993) *Explaining*, London: Routledge.

Wragg, E. C., Wikeley, F. J., Wragg, C. M. and Haynes, G. S. (1996) *Teacher Appraisal Observed,* London: Routledge.

Wragg, E. C., Wragg, C. M., Haynes, G. S. and Chamberlin, R. A. (1998) *Improving Literacy in the Primary School*, London: Routledge.

Wright, A. (1992) 'Evaluation of the first British Reading Recovery Programme', *British Educational Research Journal* **18** (4): 351–68.

Youngman, M. B. (1984) 'The nature of the new teacher's job' in E. C. Wragg (ed.) *Classroom Teaching Skills*, London: Croom Helm.

Index